D0509298

# BUN B'S

# RAP

# COLORING

# AND

# ACTIVITY

# BOOK

BY

SHEA SERRANO AND BUN B

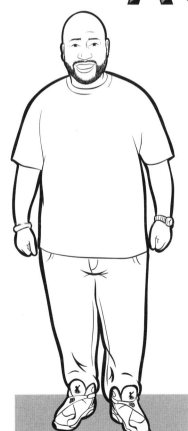

# TABLE OF CONTENTS

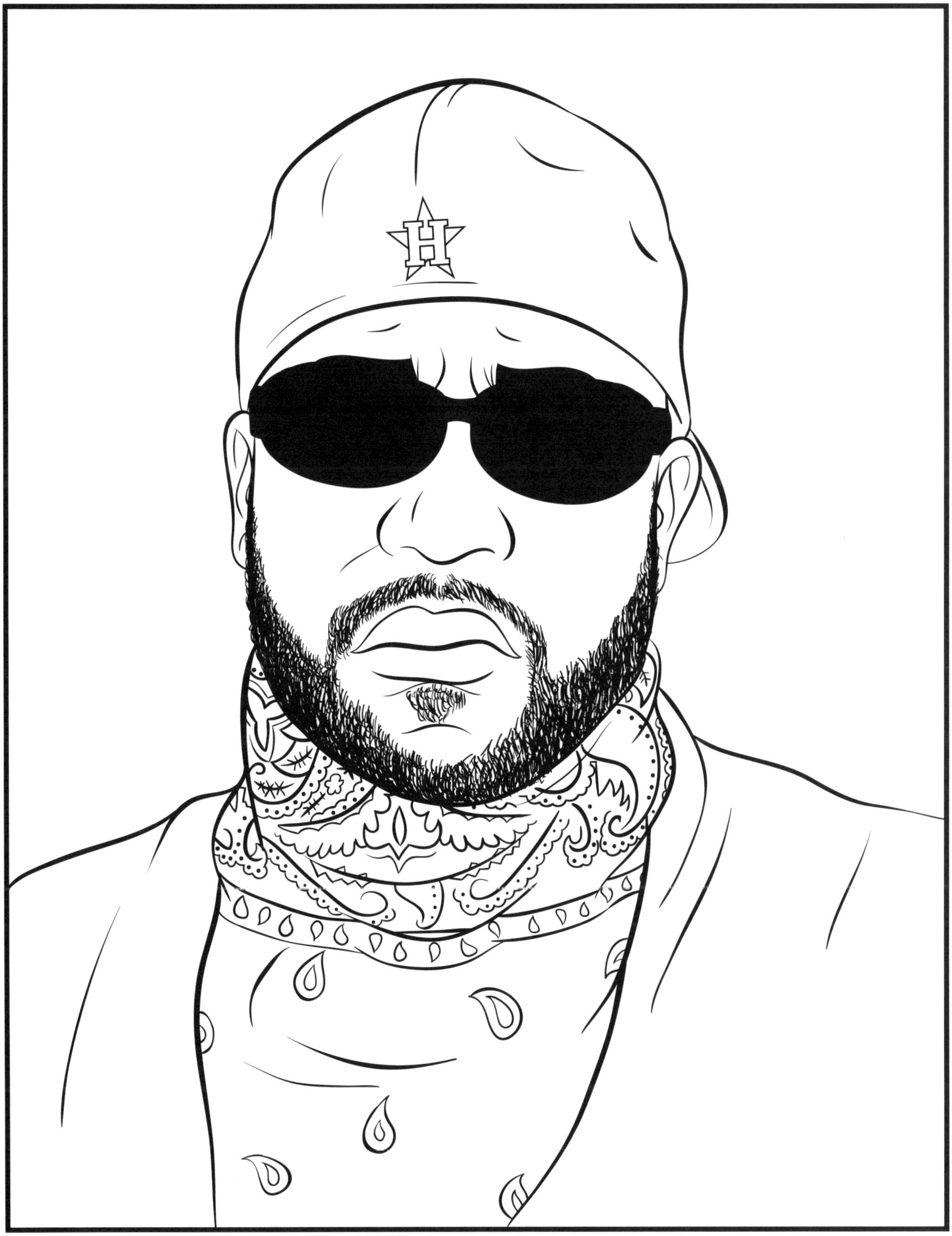

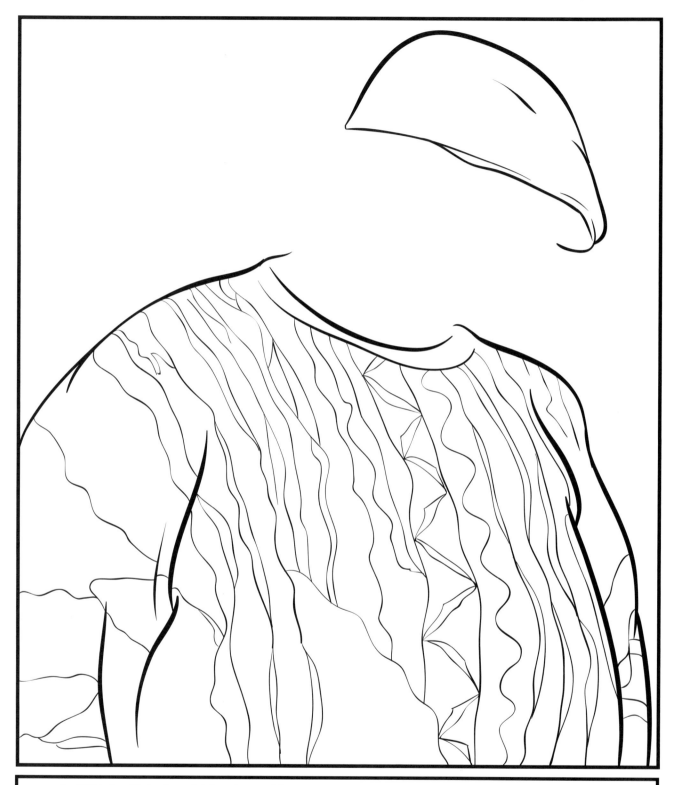

In 1994, the Notorious B.I.G. released *Ready to Die*, and rap was never quite the same again. B.I.G. was smart without being awkward, passionate without being hokey, and introspective without being corny. He's considered to be one of the greatest artists hip-hop has ever seen. Take a moment to color in his unstoppable sweater and draw in his notorious face.

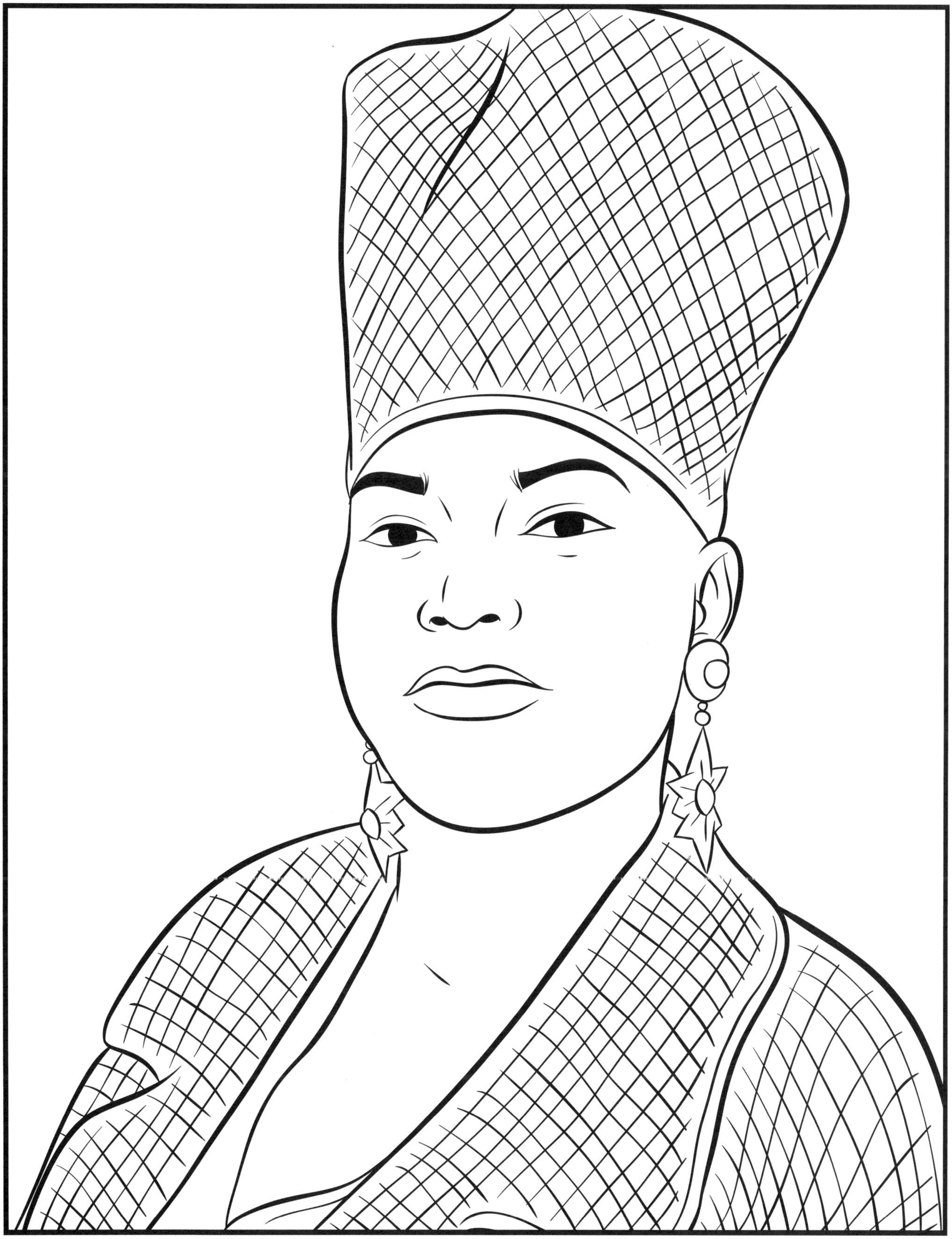

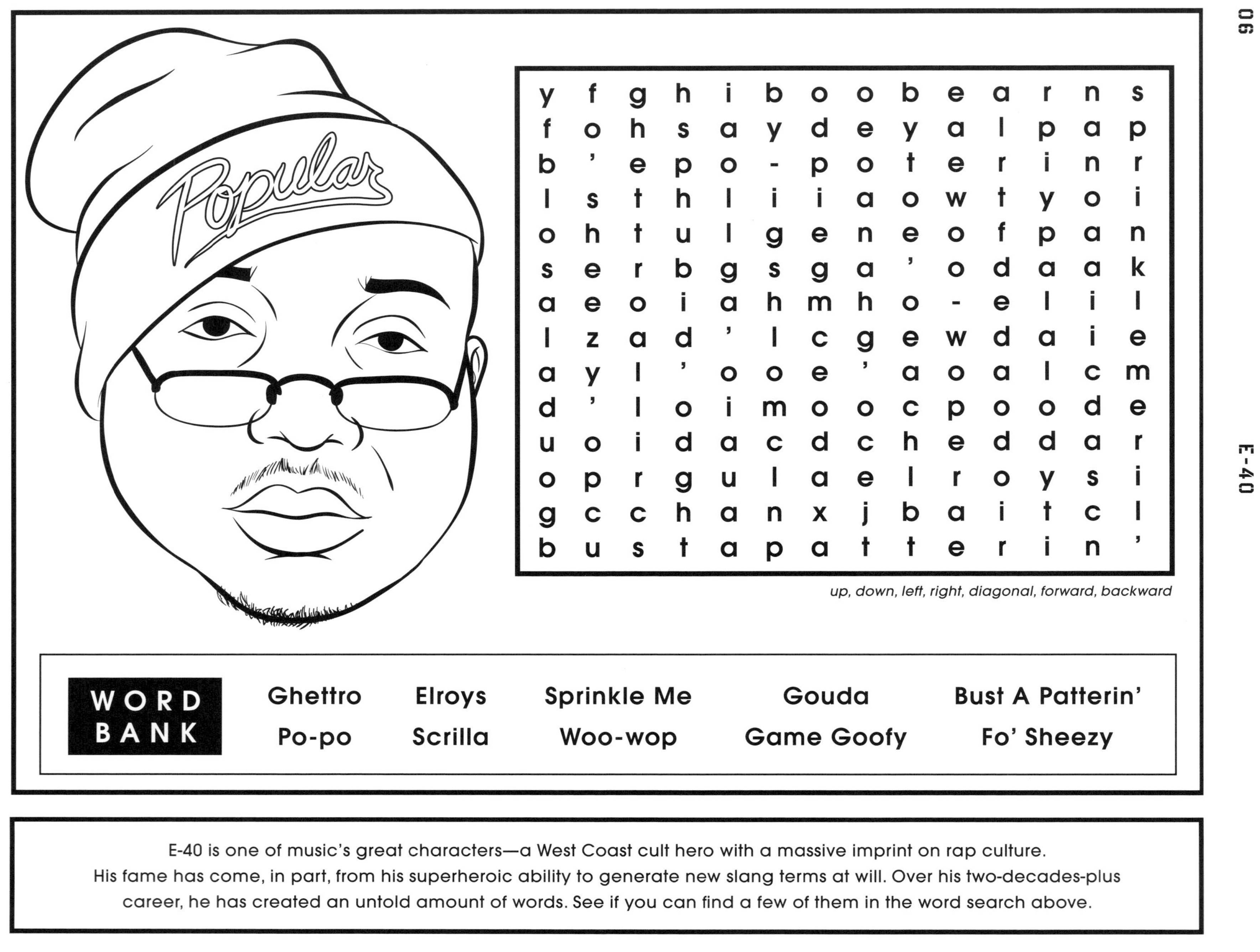
Popular

| | | | | | | | | | | | | | |
|---|---|---|---|---|---|---|---|---|---|---|---|---|---|
| y | f | g | h | i | b | o | o | b | e | a | r | n | s |
| f | o | h | s | a | y | d | e | y | a | l | p | a | p |
| b | ' | e | p | o | - | p | o | t | e | r | i | n | r |
| l | s | t | h | l | i | i | a | o | w | t | y | o | i |
| o | h | t | u | l | g | e | n | e | o | f | p | a | n |
| s | e | r | b | g | s | g | a | ' | o | d | a | a | k |
| a | e | o | i | a | h | m | h | o | - | e | l | i | l |
| l | z | a | d | ' | l | c | g | e | w | d | a | i | e |
| a | y | l | ' | o | o | e | ' | a | o | a | l | c | m |
| d | ' | l | o | i | m | o | o | c | p | o | o | d | e |
| u | o | i | d | a | c | d | c | h | e | d | d | a | r |
| o | p | r | g | u | l | a | e | l | r | o | y | s | i |
| g | c | c | h | a | n | x | j | b | a | i | t | c | l |
| b | u | s | t | a | p | a | t | t | e | r | i | n | ' |

*up, down, left, right, diagonal, forward, backward*

**WORD BANK**

| | | | | |
|---|---|---|---|---|
| Ghettro | Elroys | Sprinkle Me | Gouda | Bust A Patterin' |
| Po-po | Scrilla | Woo-wop | Game Goofy | Fo' Sheezy |

E-40 is one of music's great characters—a West Coast cult hero with a massive imprint on rap culture. His fame has come, in part, from his superheroic ability to generate new slang terms at will. Over his two-decades-plus career, he has created an untold amount of words. See if you can find a few of them in the word search above.

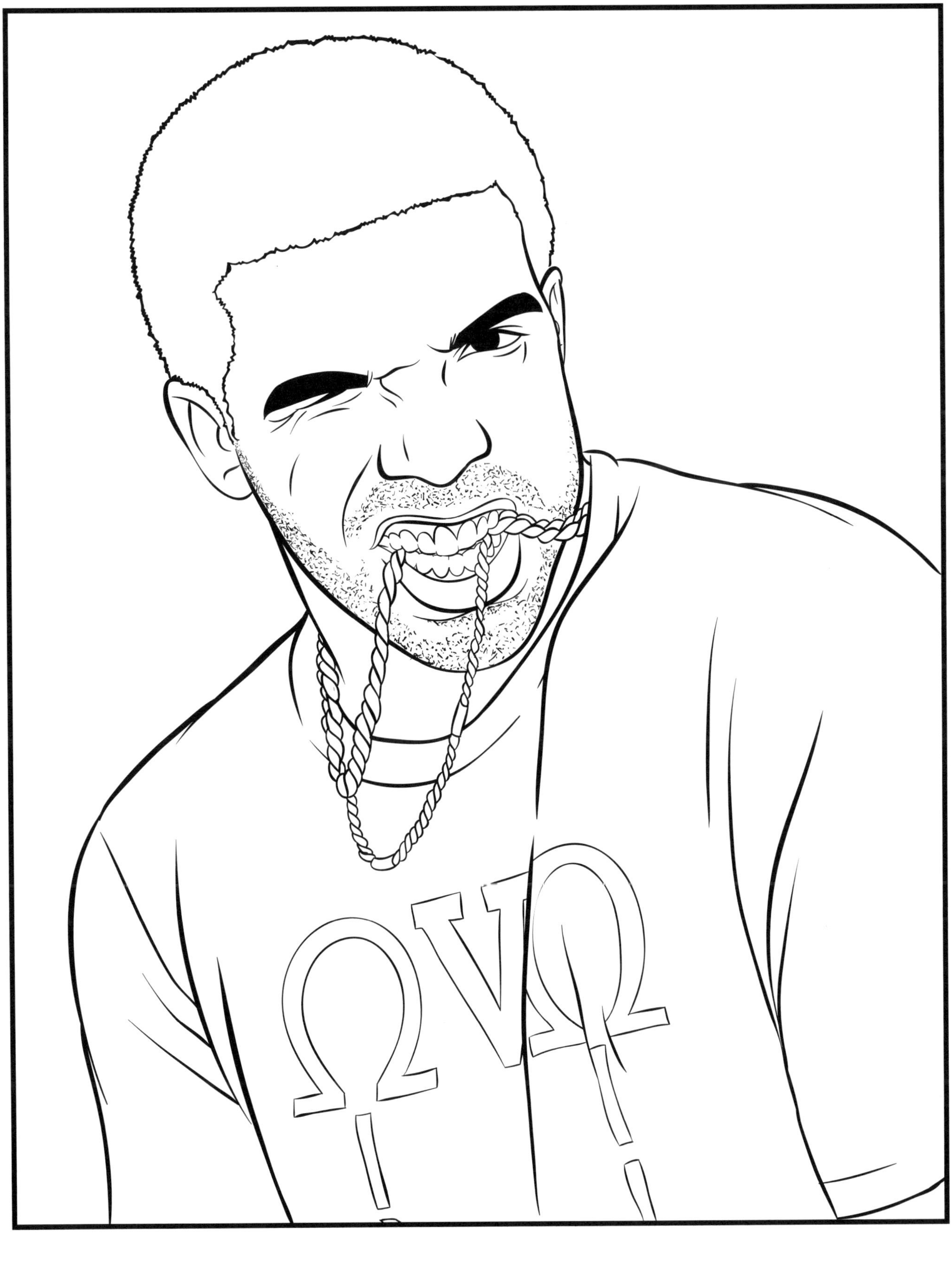

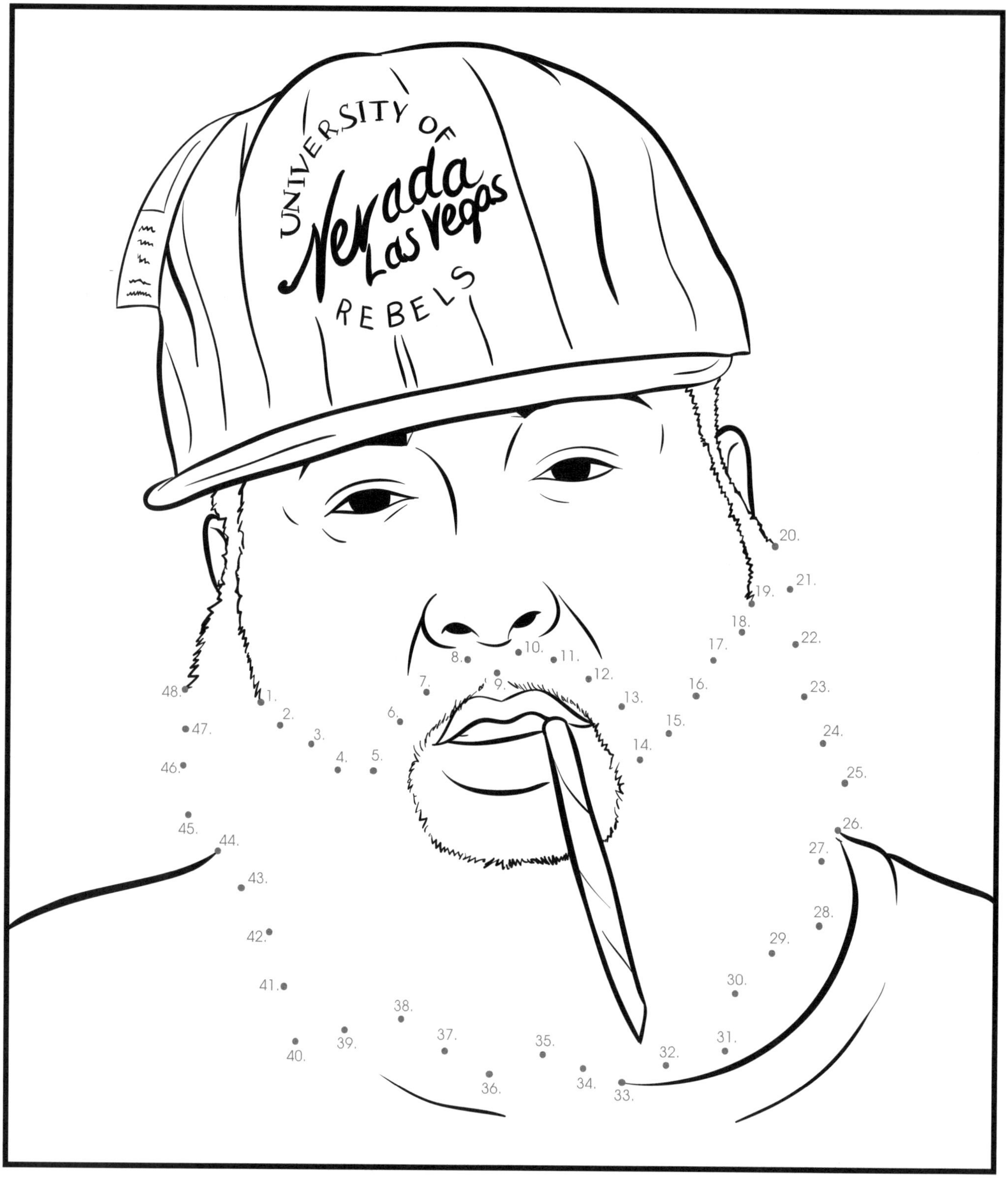
UNIVERSITY OF
Nevada
Las Vegas
REBELS
1.
2.
3.
4.
5.
6.
7.
8.
9.
10.
11.
12.
13.
14.
15.
16.
17.
18.
19.
20.
21.
22.
23.
24.
25.
26.
27.
28.
29.
30.
31.
32.
33.
34.
35.
36.
37.
38.
39.
40.
41.
42.
43.
44.
45.
46.
47.
48.

Run–D.M.C. has the Adidas. Flavor Flav has the clock. Lil Wayne has the dreads. And Action Bronson has his beard. Or, rather, he usually does. Connect the dots above to fill it in for him.

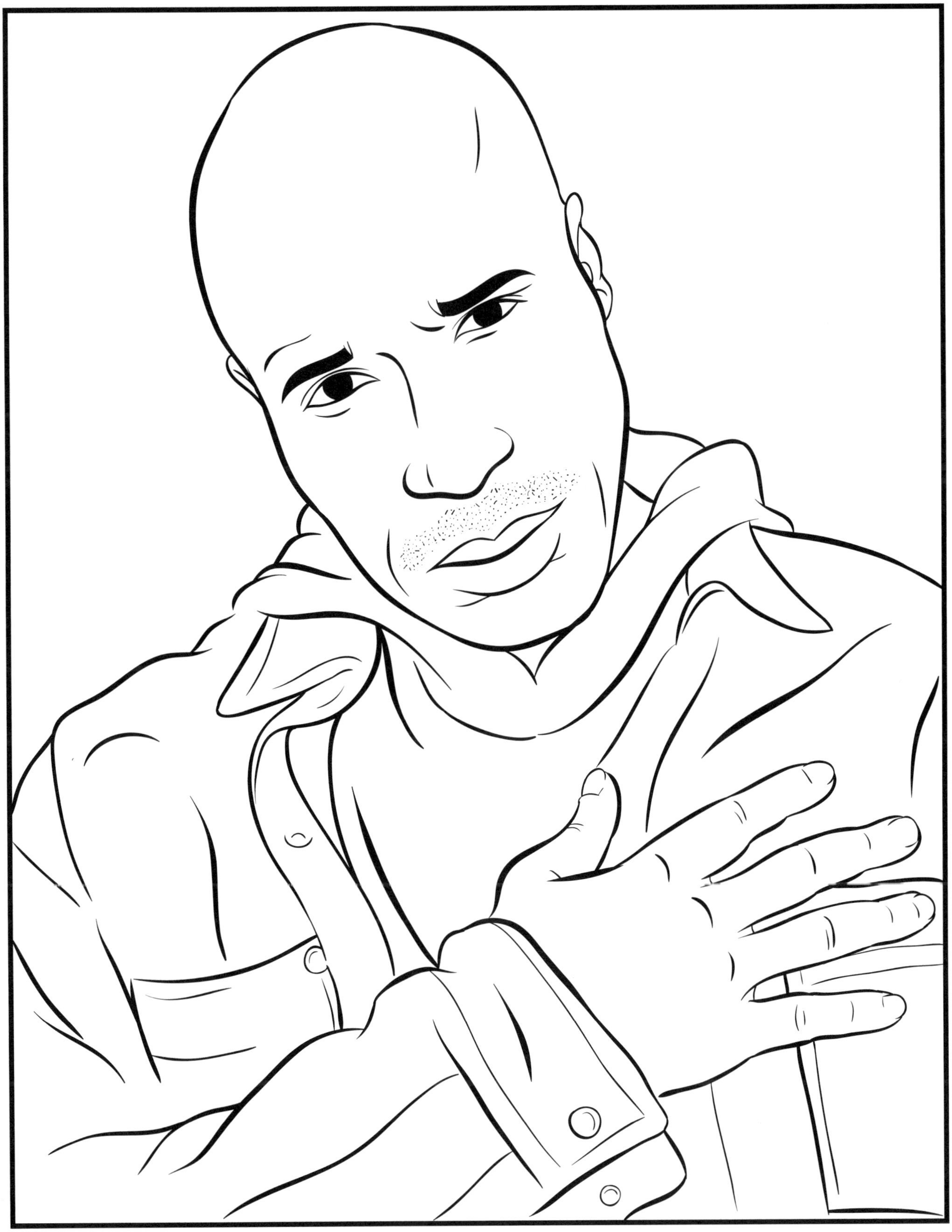

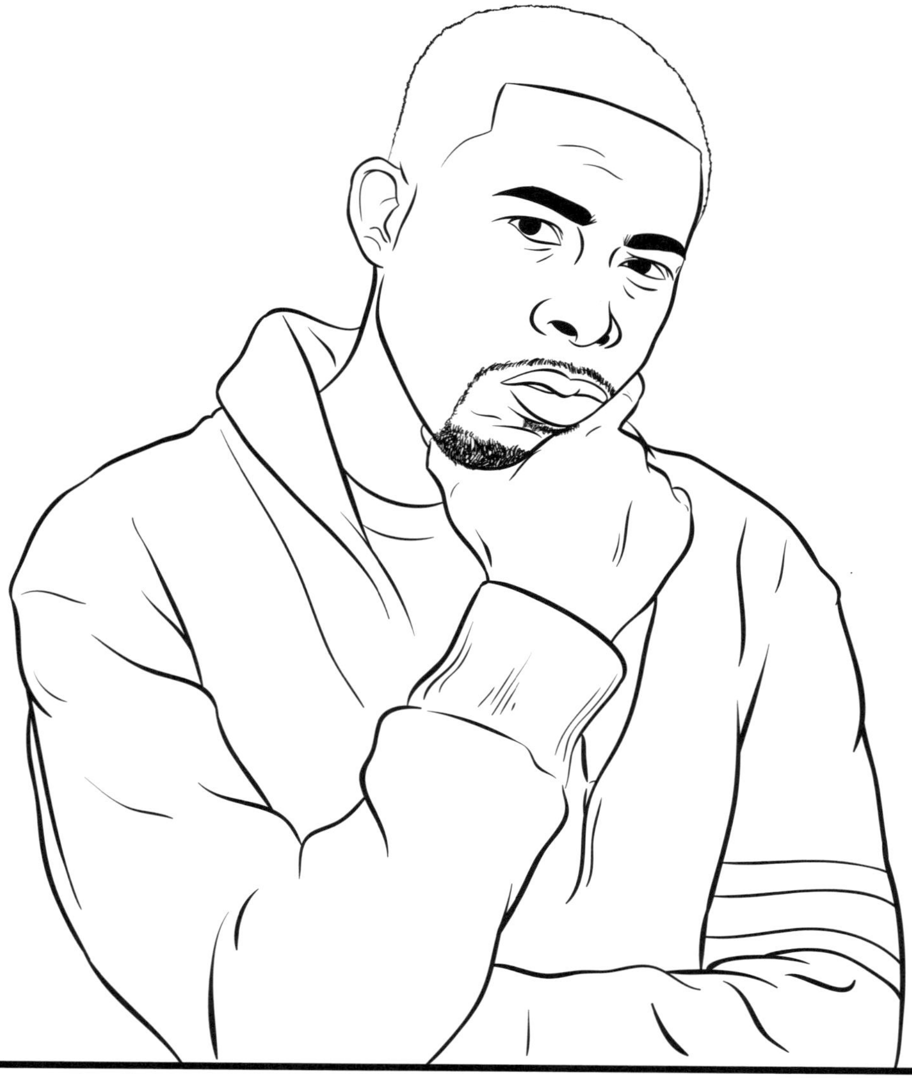

## Brain Boxing with the Genius

The Big Bang Theory predicted the dilation of distant light source curves. Has that been observed yet?

If we are to concede that the universe is, in fact, expanding, then the follow-up question is obvious: What is the universe expanding into?

If we are not to concede that the universe is expanding, then, by elimination, that would mean that our definitions of length and time are changing, right?

In addition to being one of the greatest rappers of all time, GZA, otherwise known as the Genius, is also one of the most cerebral and contemplative. He's currently trying to unravel the mysteries of the universe. See if you can keep up with him by answering a few basic cosmological questions.

ANSWERS 1.?, 2.?, 3.? Sorry.

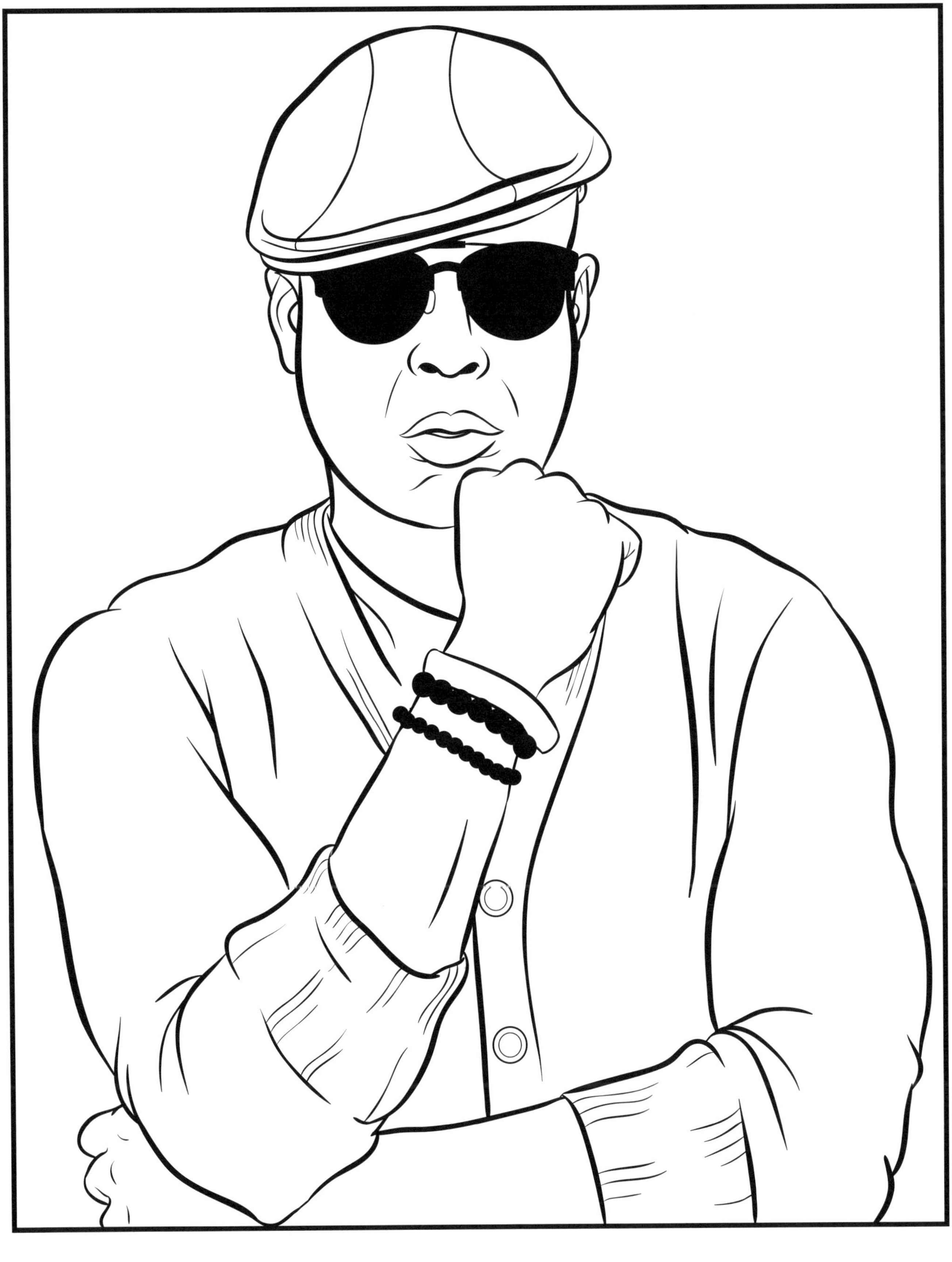

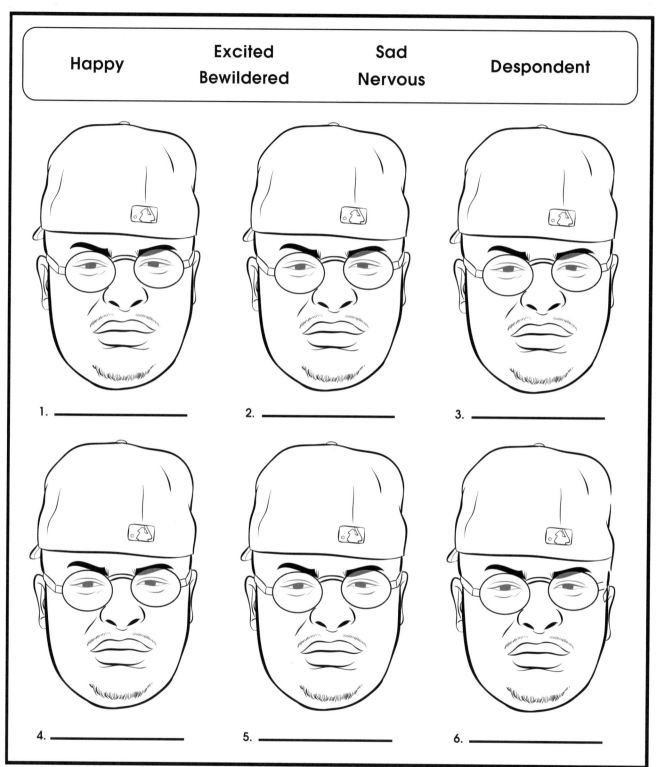

| | | | |
|---|---|---|---|
| Happy | Excited<br>Bewildered | Sad<br>Nervous | Despondent |

1. ____________

2. ____________

3. ____________

4. ____________

5. ____________

6. ____________

Scarface has long possessed one of rap's most unnerving, impenetrable stares.
Can you figure out what he's feeling?

ANSWERS 1. Happy, 2. Sad, 3. Bewildered, 4. Nervous, 5. Despondent, 6. Excited

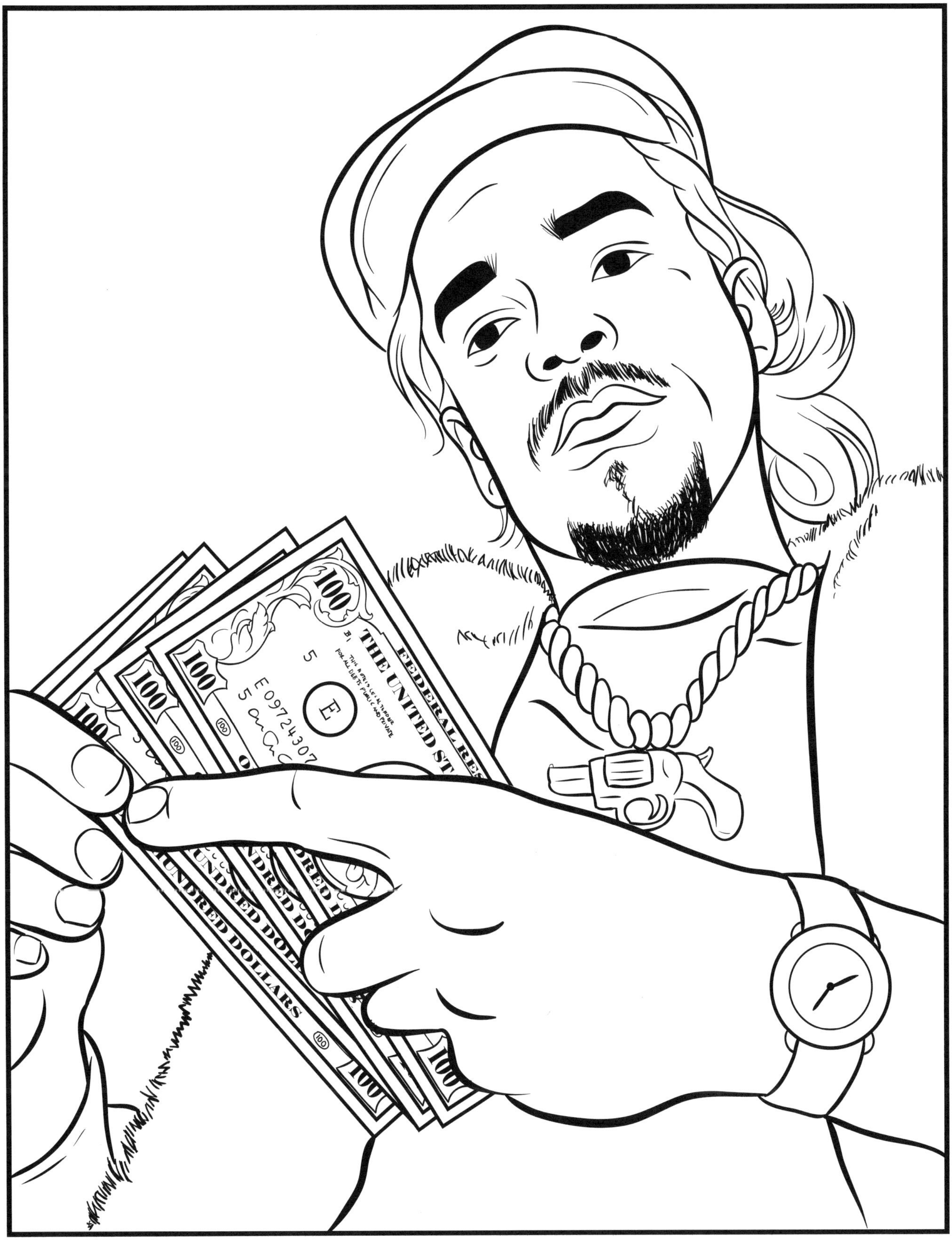
100
FEDERAL RES
THE UNITED ST
UNDRED DOLLARS

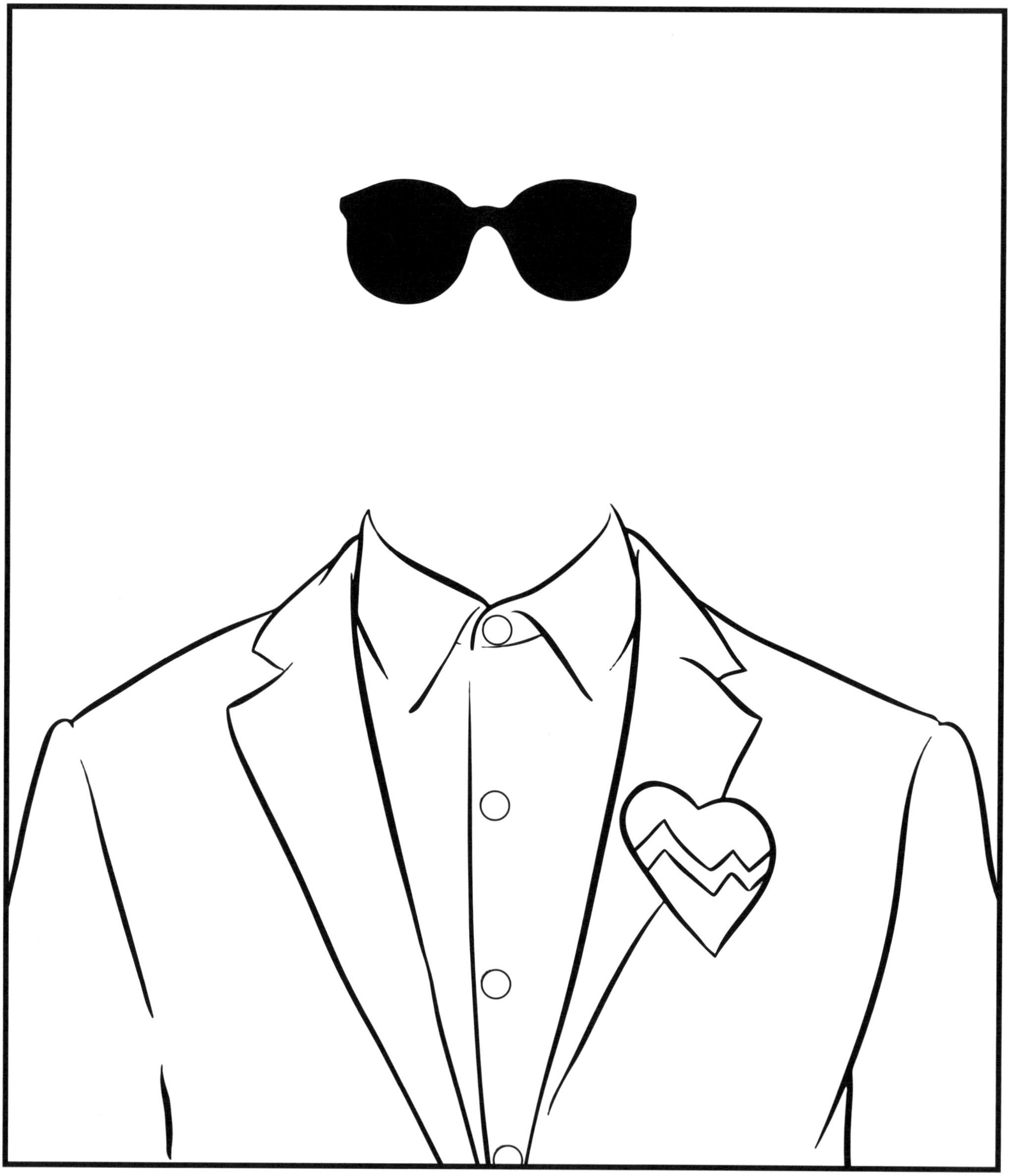

To match the robotic angst of his fourth album, *808s & Heartbreak*, promo material was sent out with Kanye West wearing what has aged to become the most important gray glen plaid suit in all of hip-hop. Kanye's in love now, so he doesn't need it anymore. Draw someone else in it.

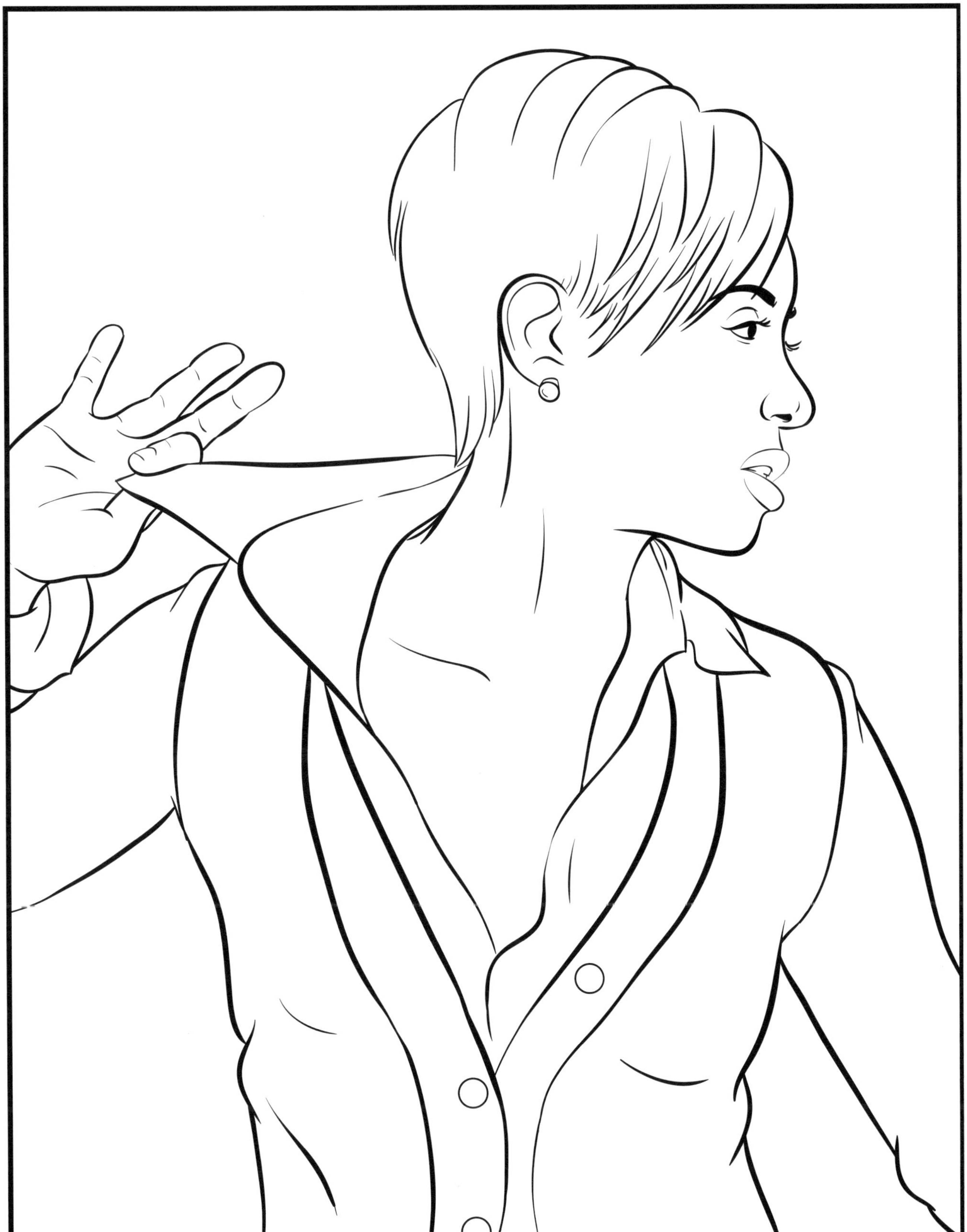

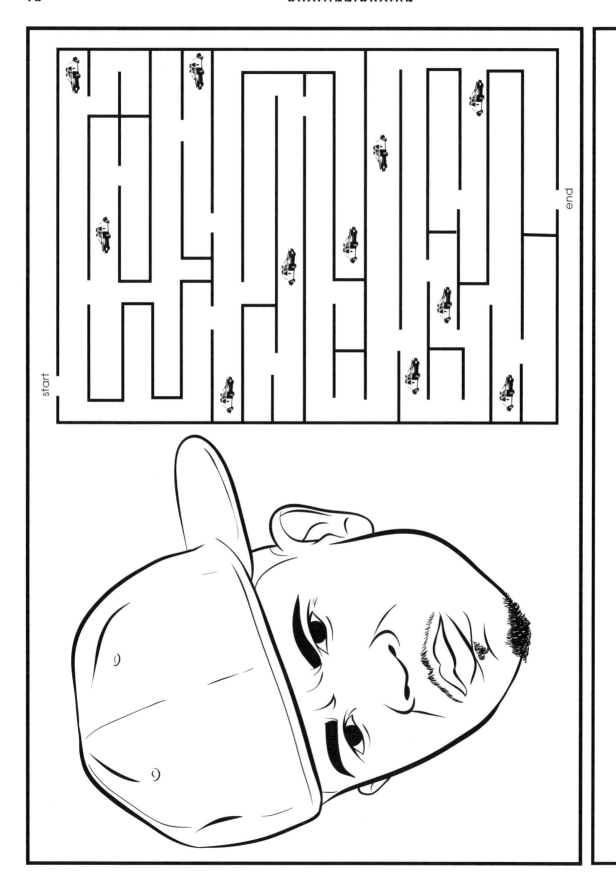

start

end

The police have seen Chamillionaire rolling. They're hating, patrolling, and trying to catch him riding dirty. Can you help him get to his destination without running into law enforcement?

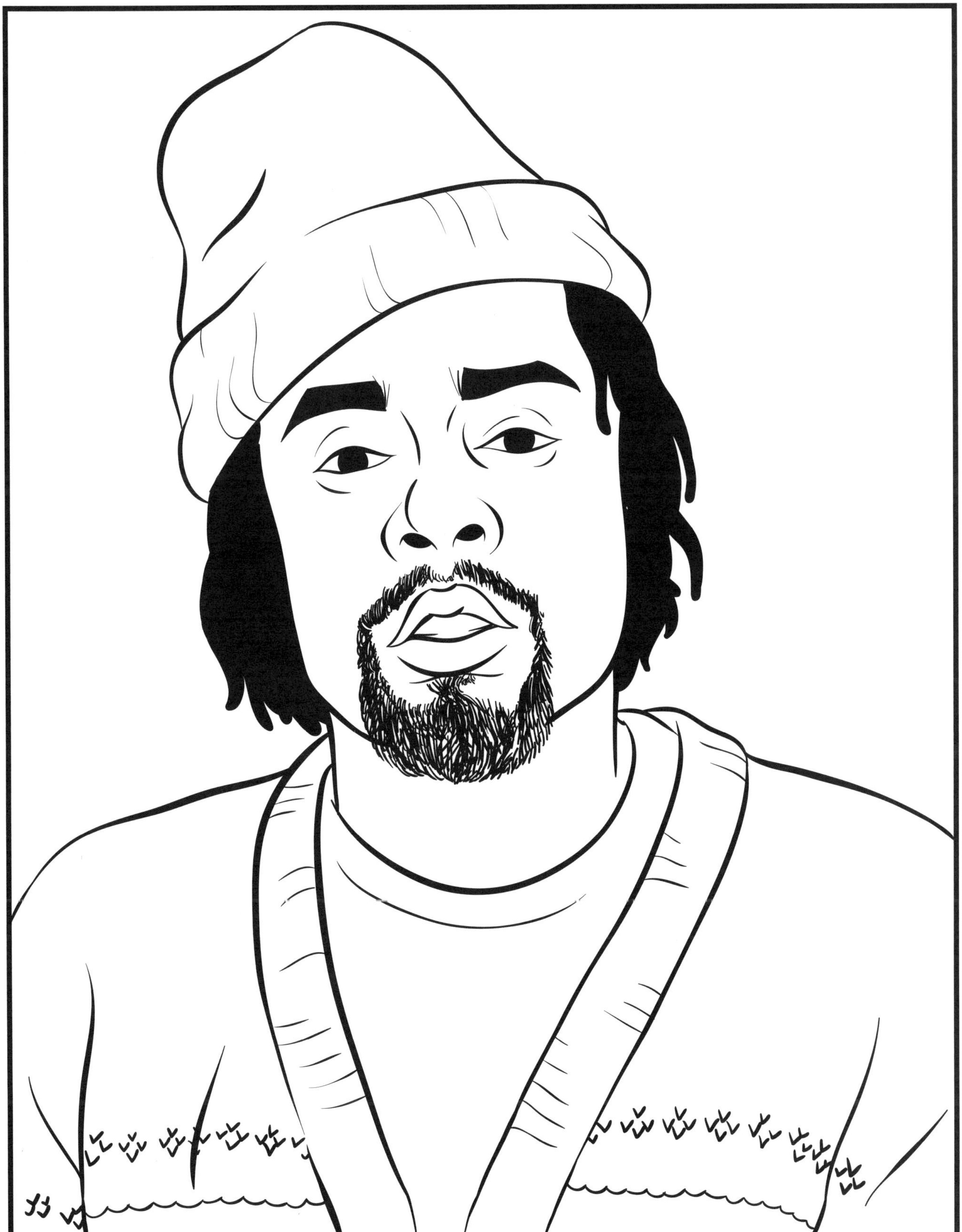

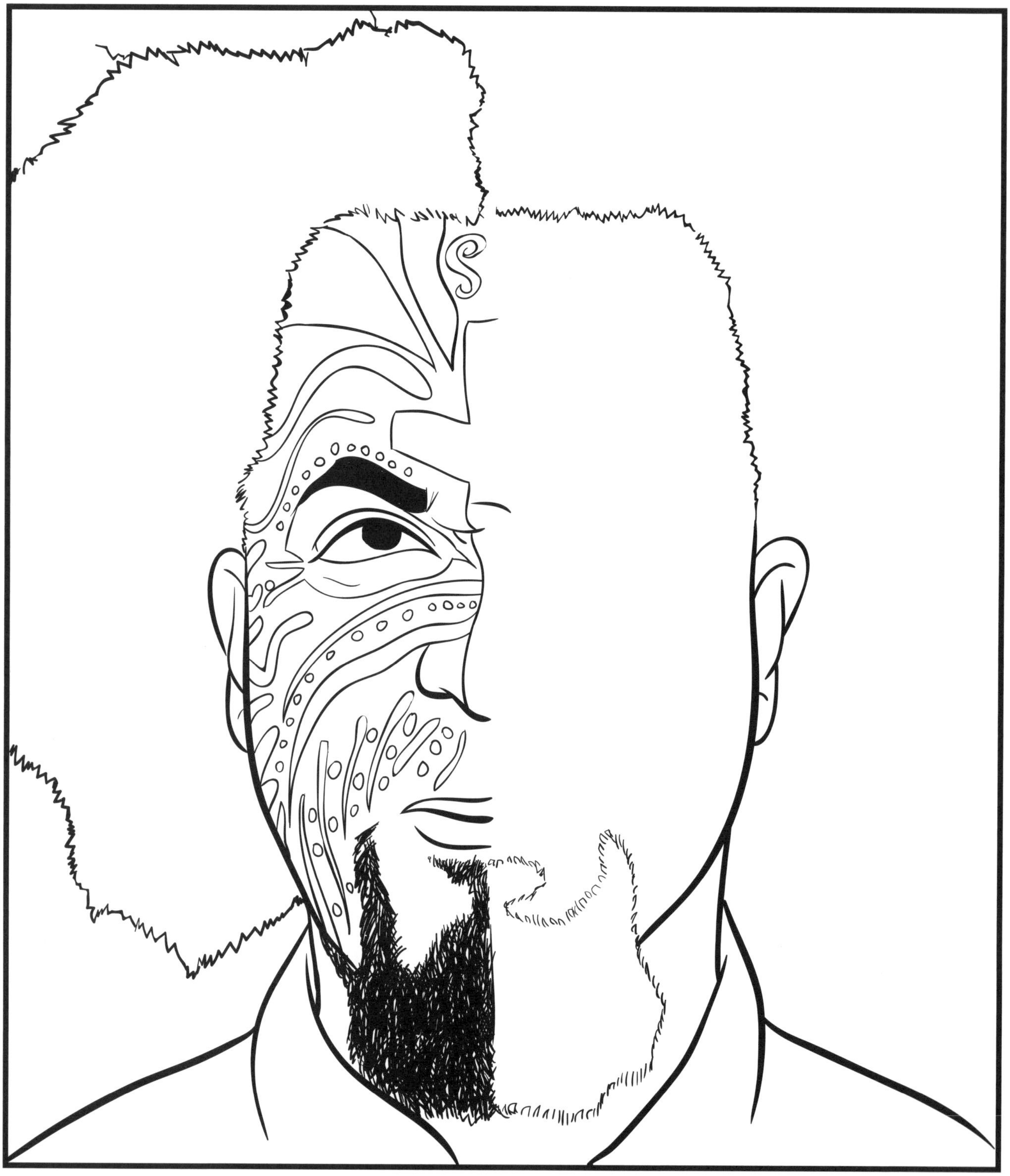

Few rappers have explored the inside of their own brains more fearlessly or creatively than Tech N9ne, a trait that bleeds out from his albums onto his actual album artwork. See if you can complete the missing side of his face from 2009's *Sickology 101* cover.

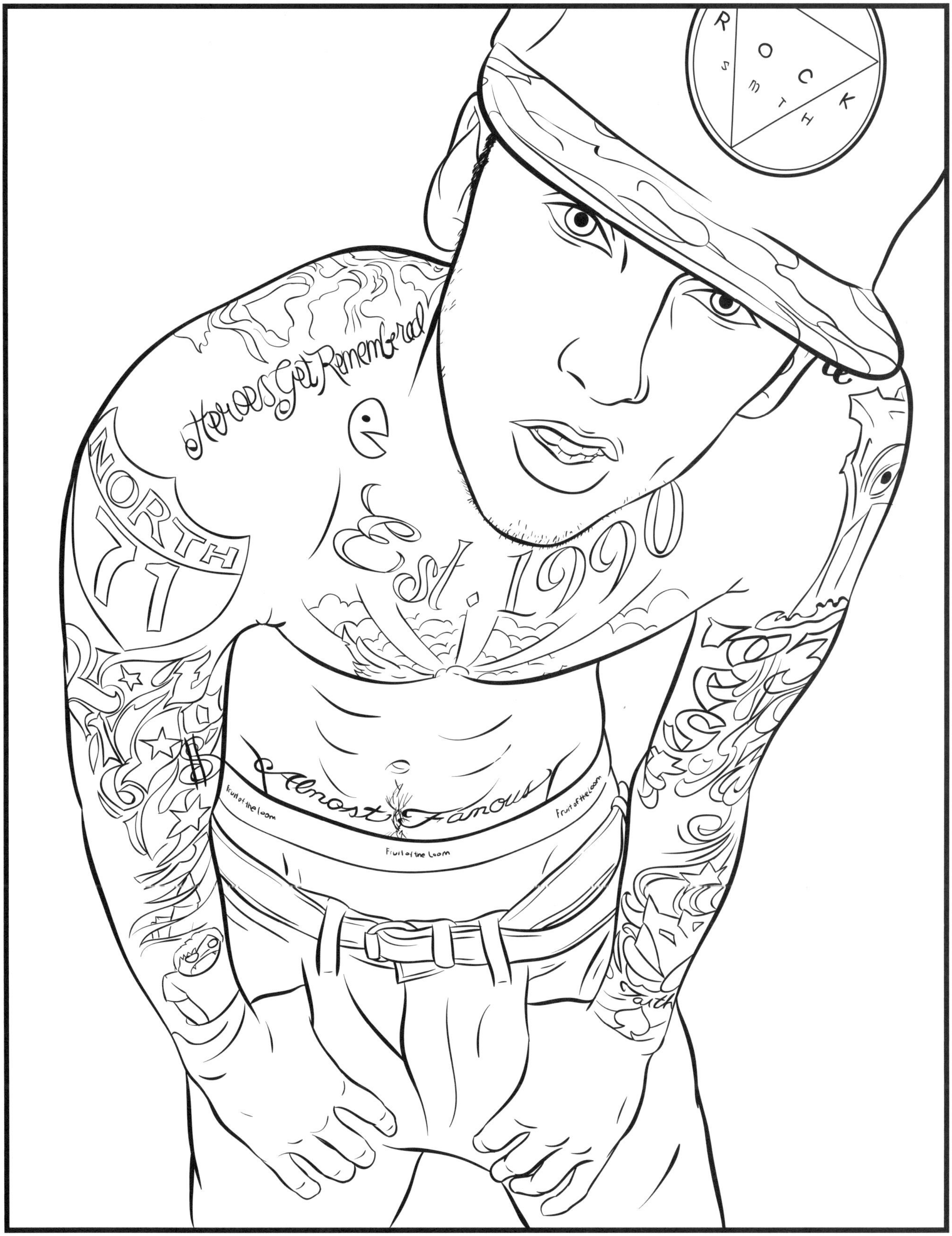
ROCK
SMTH
Heroes Get Remembered
NORTH
71
Est. 1990
Almost Famous
Fruit of the Loom
Fruit of the Loom
Fruit of the Loom

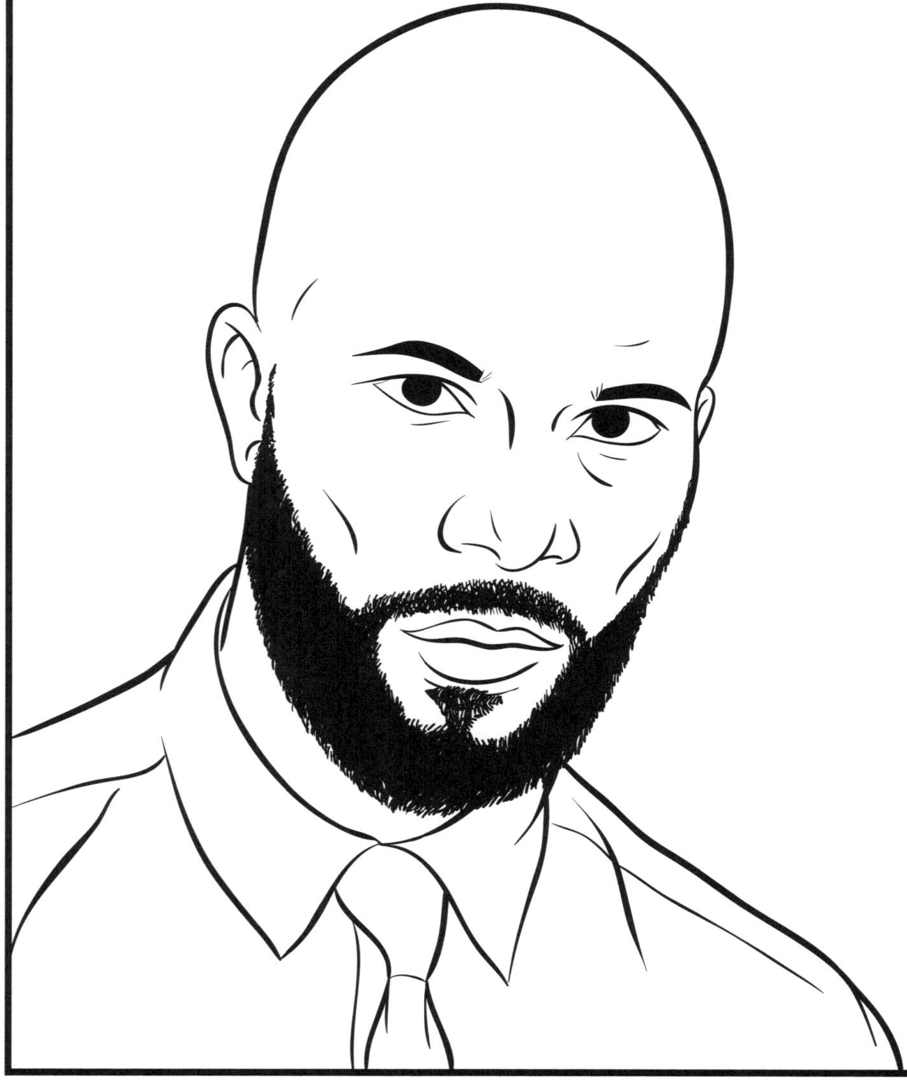

## True or False: The Questions

1. Why do these girls look so good in the summer? ______

2. 'Cause you answer the phone "peace," that mean you ain't a freak? ______

3. You know it was a mistake introducing me to your girlfriend, right? Like, I mean, look at me. ______

4. Did you see me in The Wanted? Good stuff, right? ______

5. Why did Dr. J shave his beard and mustache? ______

6. 'Cause you recognize me, yo, I gotta speak? ______

7. If I'm an intellectual, I can't be sexual? ______

8. Why do I need I.D. to get I.D.? ______

9. Do you have soy milk instead? ______

10. Now you know yo' stomach too big to be wearin' a shirt like that. So why you wanna go and do that? ______

In 2000, Common released *Like Water for Chocolate*, an album largely considered to be a brilliant bit of emotive, honest lyricism. The seventh song on it, "The Questions," sees Common and Mos Def toss questions out into the open air for examination. Play True or False above to see if you can identify questions that weren't asked.

ANSWERS 1. T, 2. T, 3. F, 4. F, 5. T, 6. T, 7. T, 8. T, 9. F, 10. T

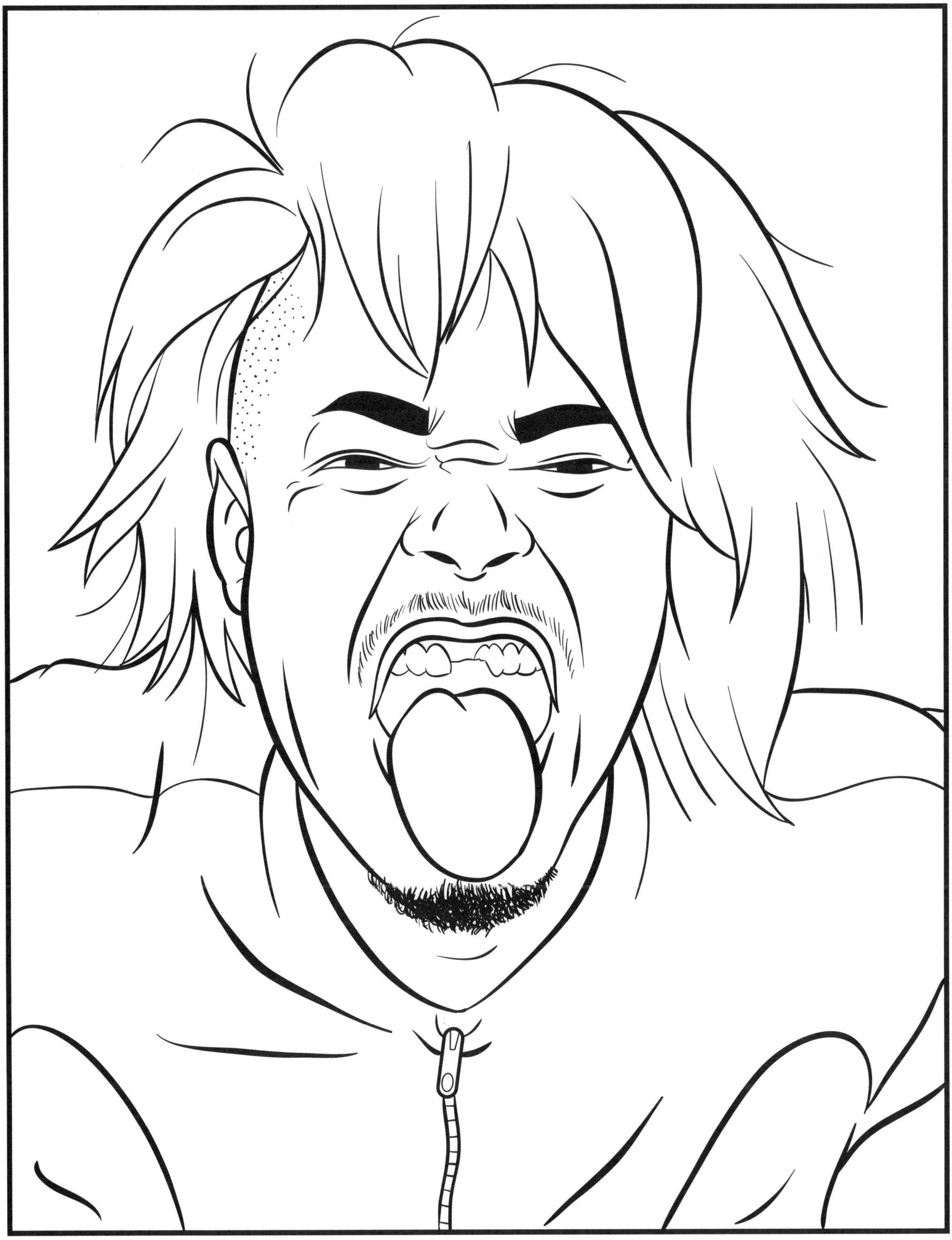

**RiFF RAFF Coloring Key**

Skin: Tan
Eyes: Green/Gray
Ring: Gold
Teeth: Gold
Earring: Gold
Snake Bracelet: Yellow
Hair: Light brown
Braids: Dark brown
Undershirt: Pink
Necklace: Black
Shirt: Every other color

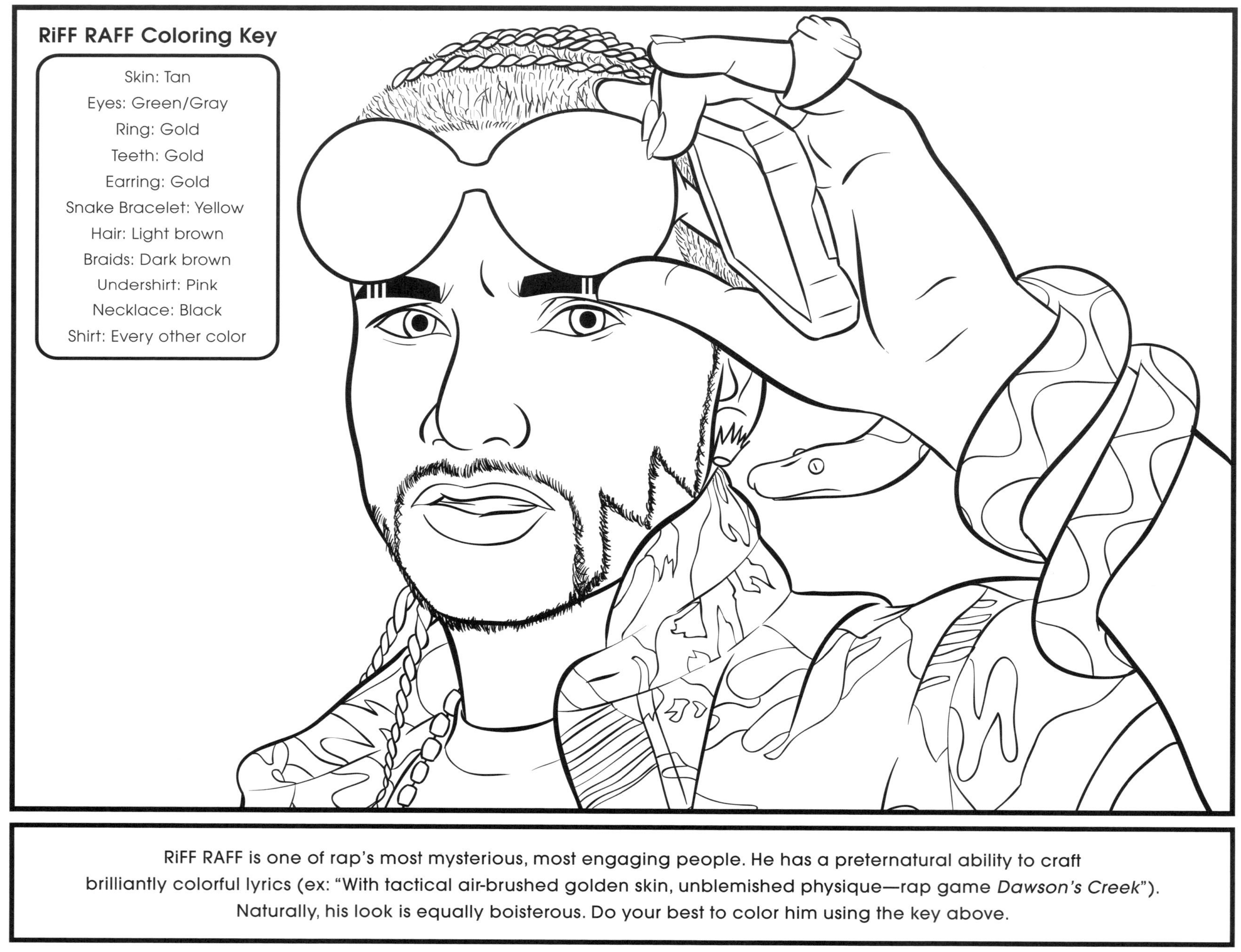

RiFF RAFF is one of rap's most mysterious, most engaging people. He has a preternatural ability to craft brilliantly colorful lyrics (ex: "With tactical air-brushed golden skin, unblemished physique—rap game *Dawson's Creek*"). Naturally, his look is equally boisterous. Do your best to color him using the key above.

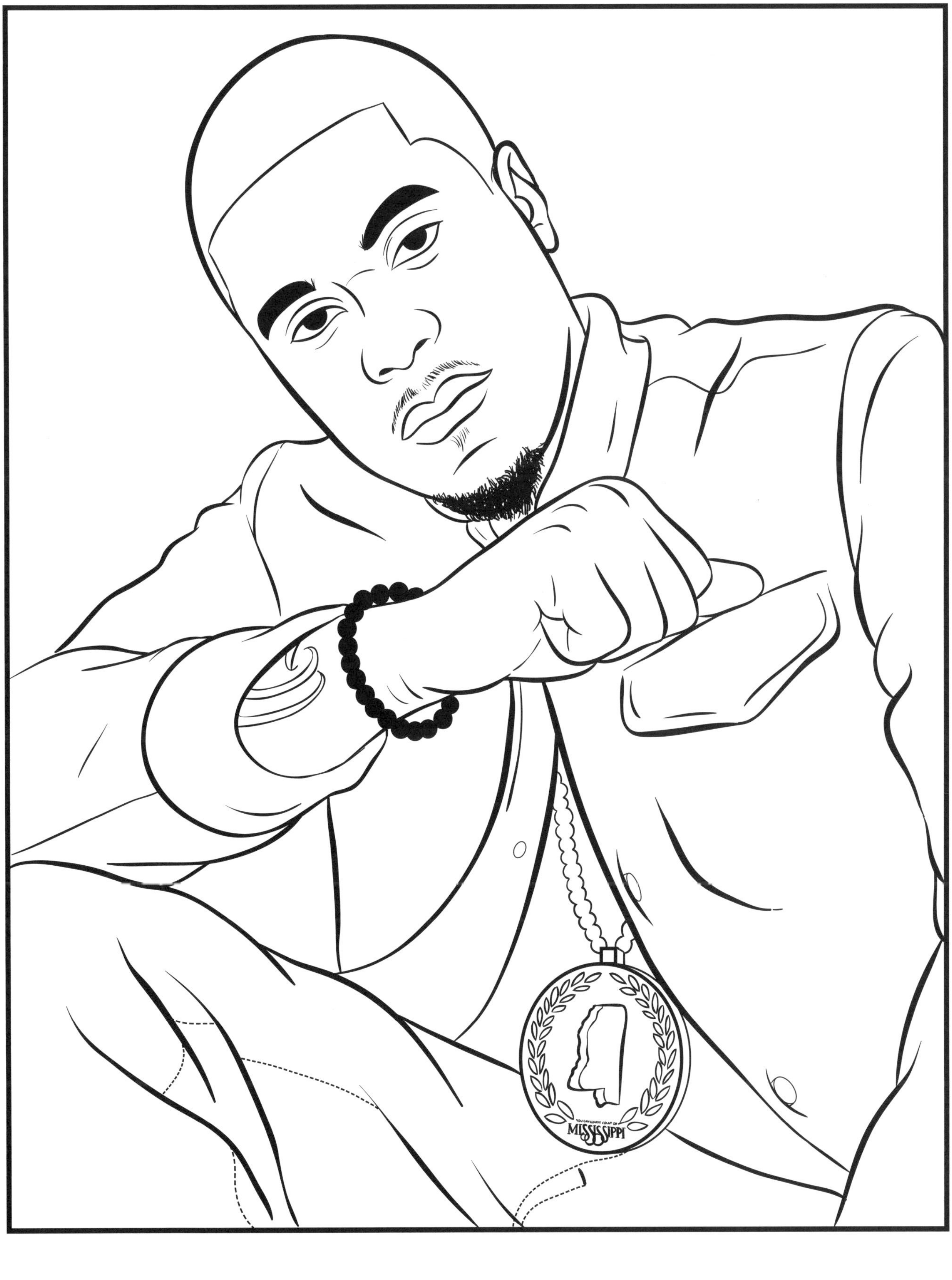
MISSISSIPPI

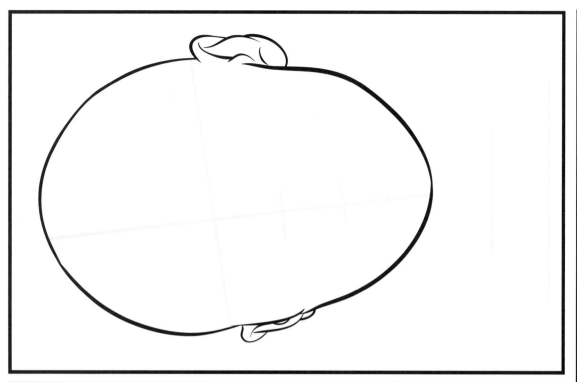

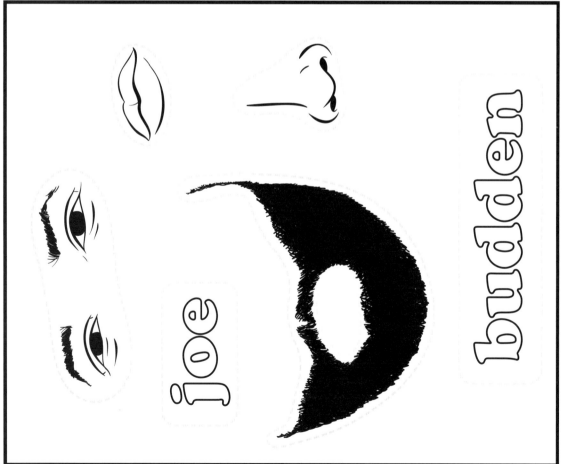

Joe Budden is a dexterous lyricist and an imaginative songwriter. When he's at his very best, it can seem less like he's human and more like he's some sort of super rap cyborg that's been crafted by scientists. Cut out the pieces on the left and paste them to the face on the right to see if you can build a Budden.

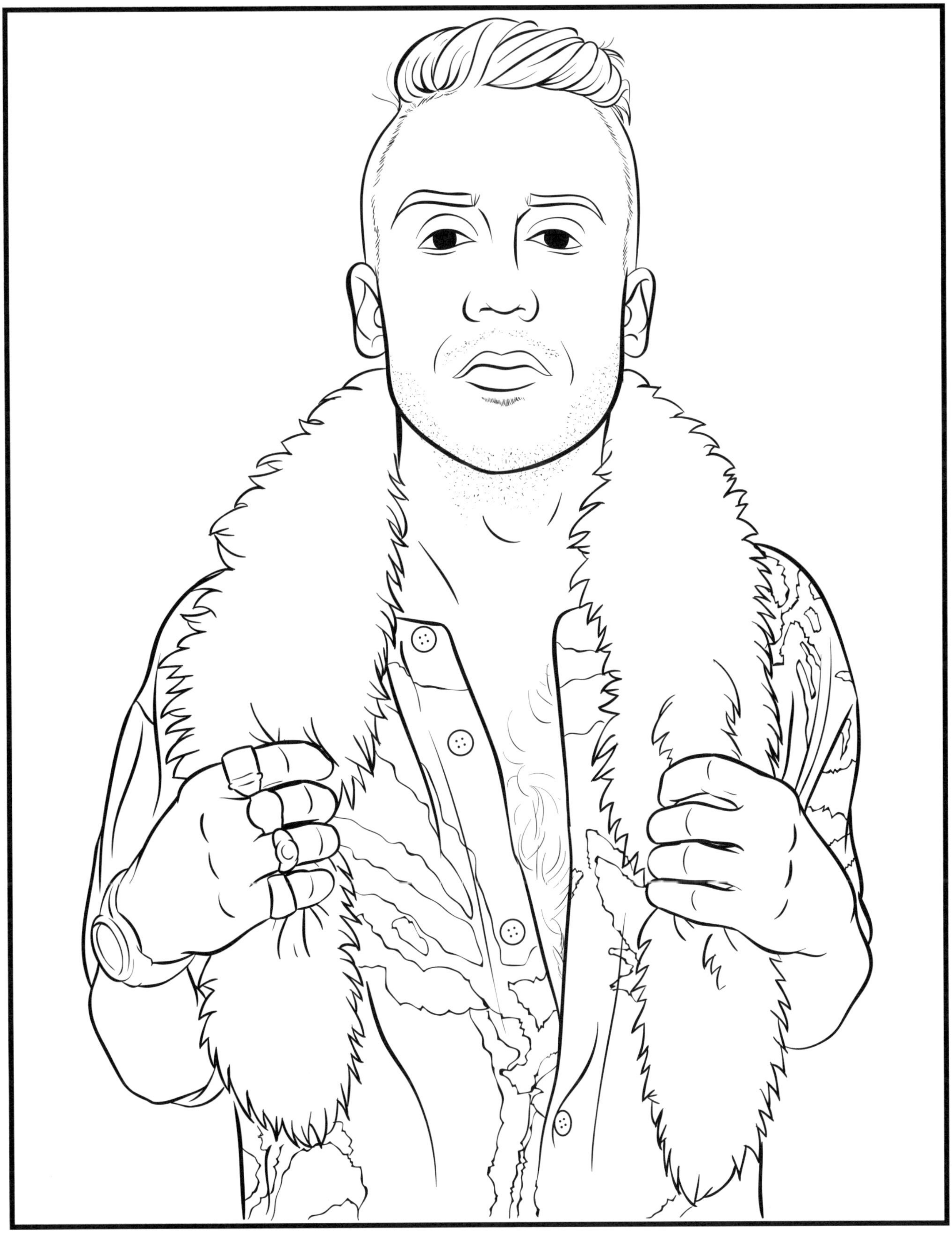

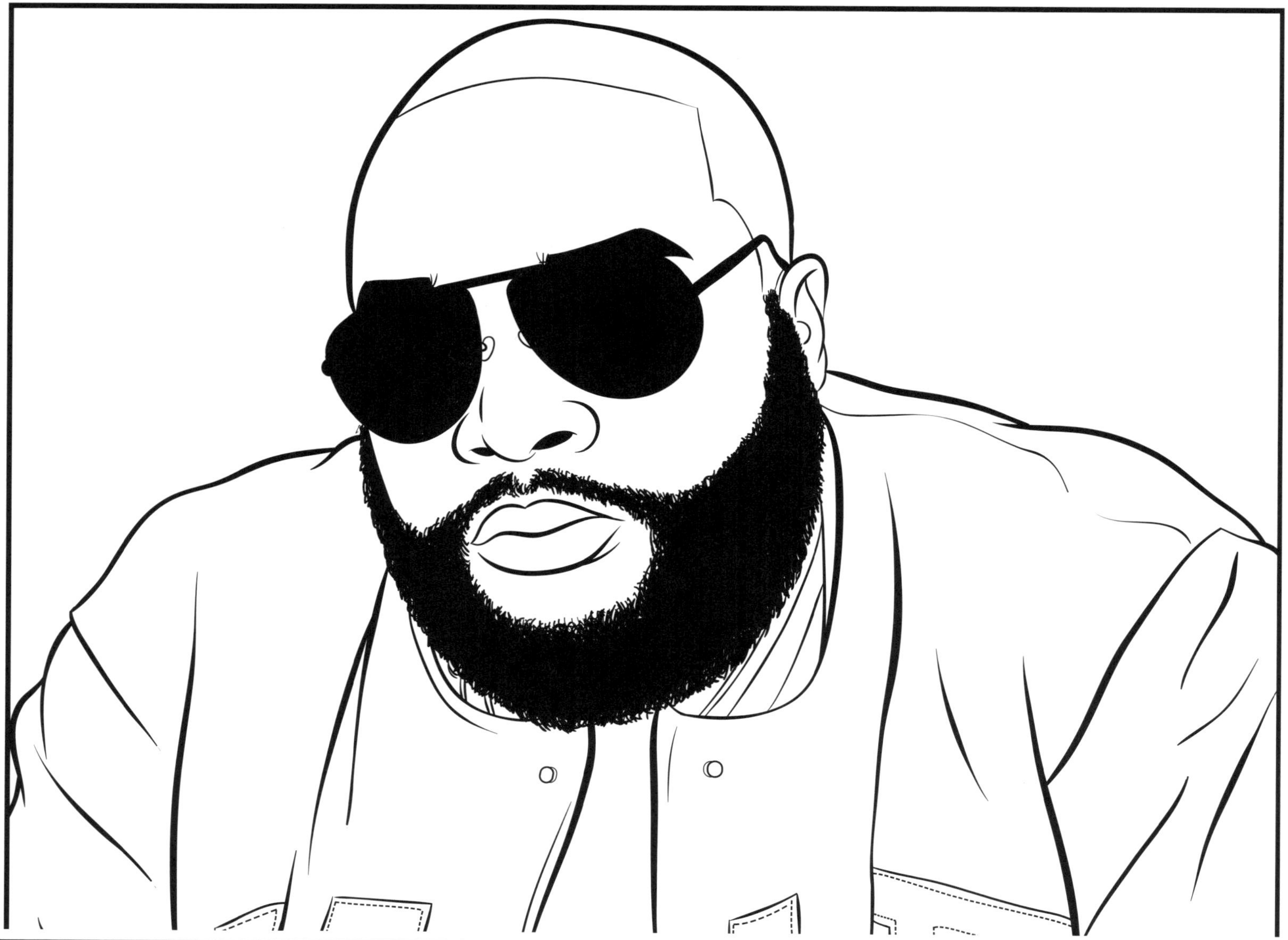

Few in history have ever manufactured, streamlined, and then crystallized a rap persona as perfectly (and effectively) as Florida's megastar Rick Ross. Since the release of 2006's *Port of Miami*, Ross has built himself into one of music's most irrepressibly sucessful forces. Here, though, despite his assertion on 2013's "Hold Me Back," it appears his haters have momentarily won: They've managed to hold his face back! Can you draw it in for him?

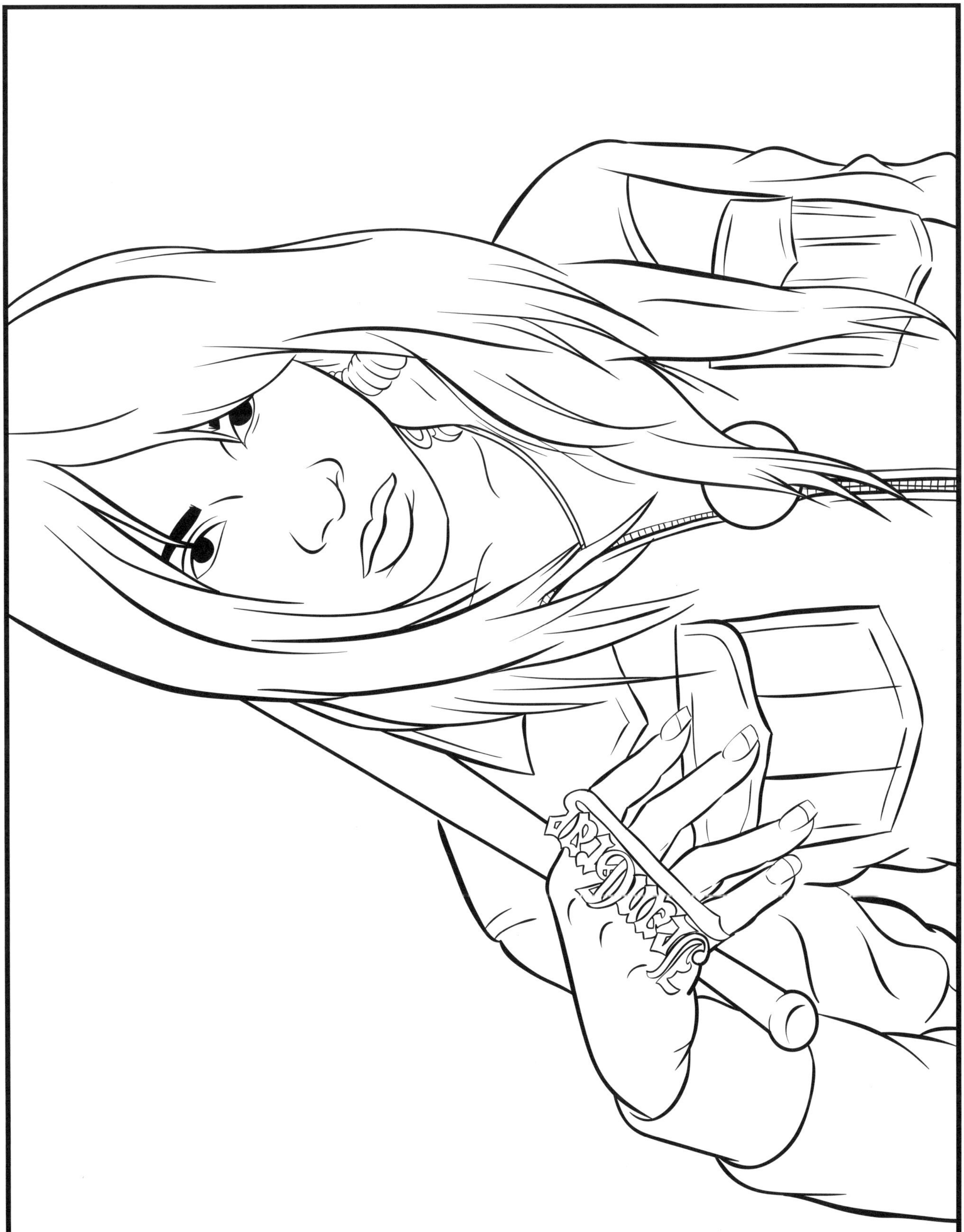

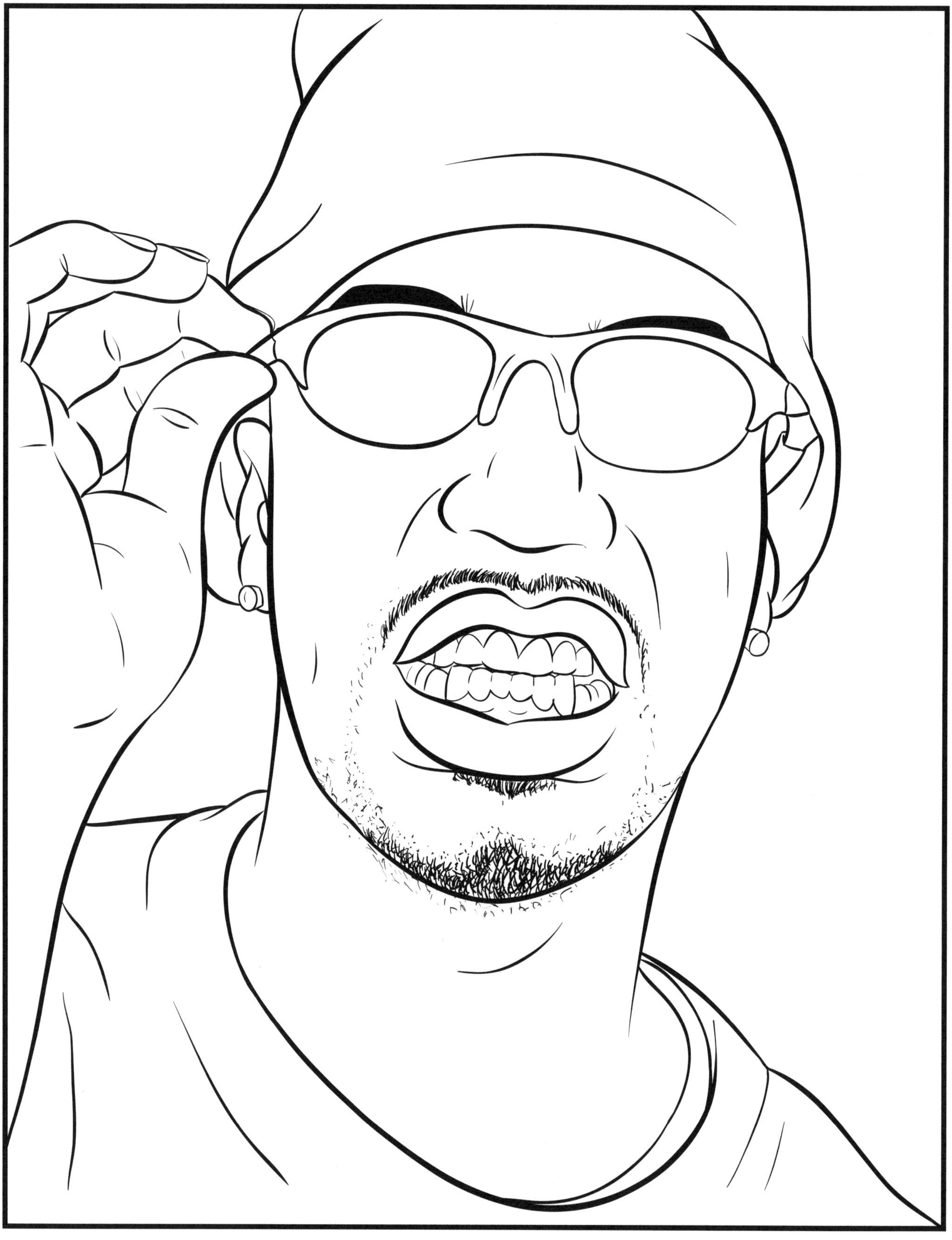

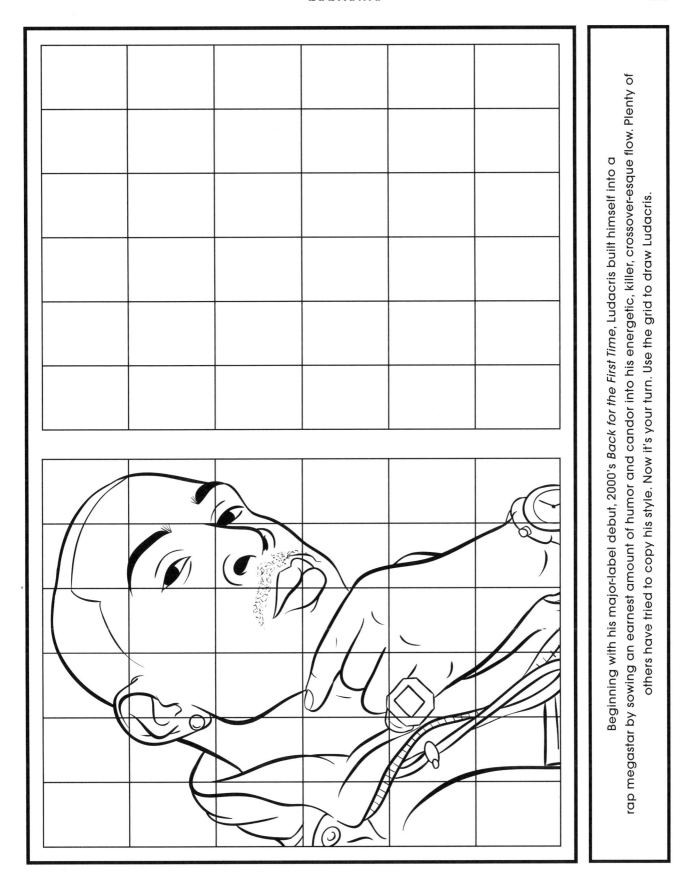

Beginning with his major-label debut, 2000's *Back for the First Time*, Ludacris built himself into a rap megastar by sowing an earnest amount of humor and candor into his energetic, killer, crossover-esque flow. Plenty of others have tried to copy his style. Now it's your turn. Use the grid to draw Ludacris.

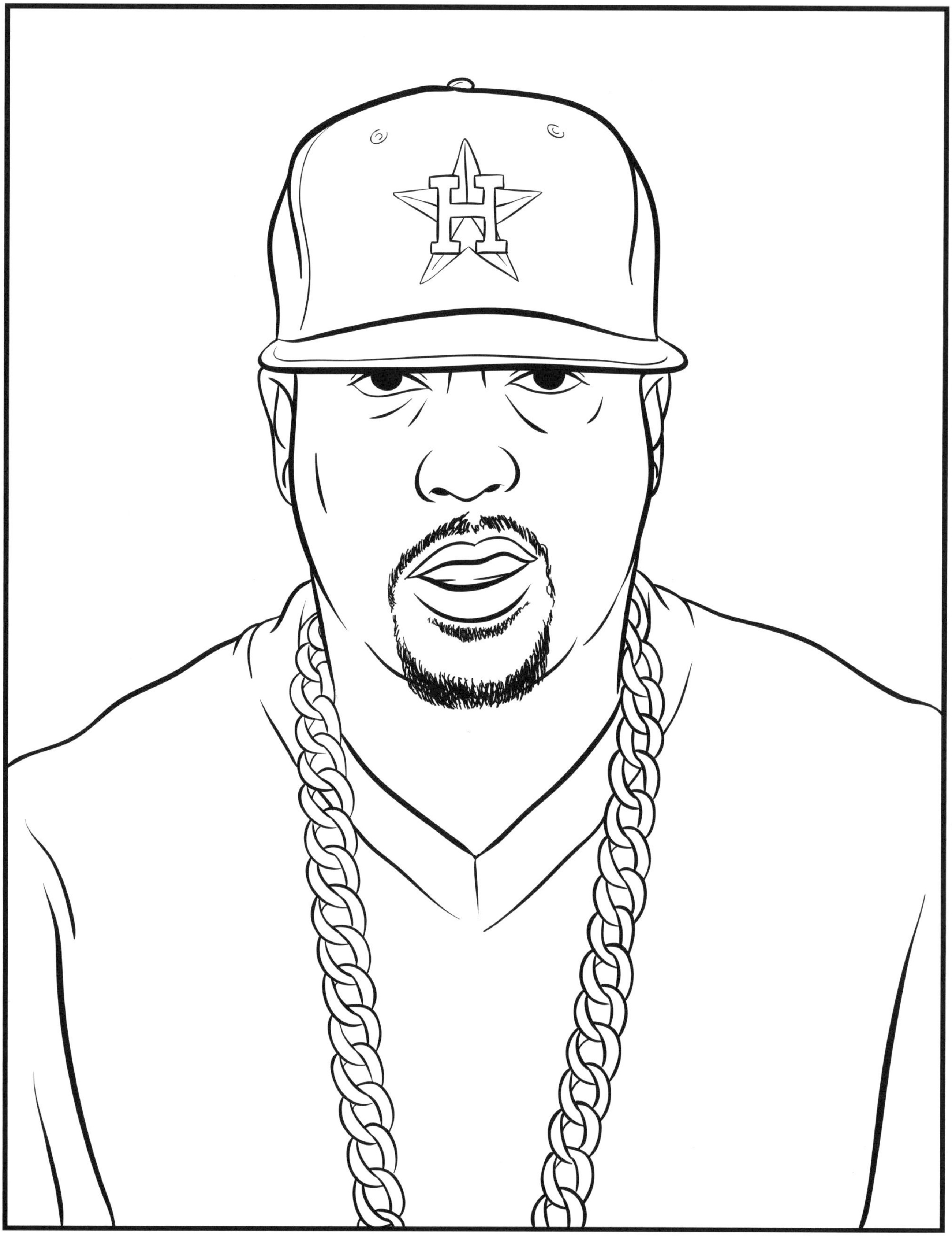

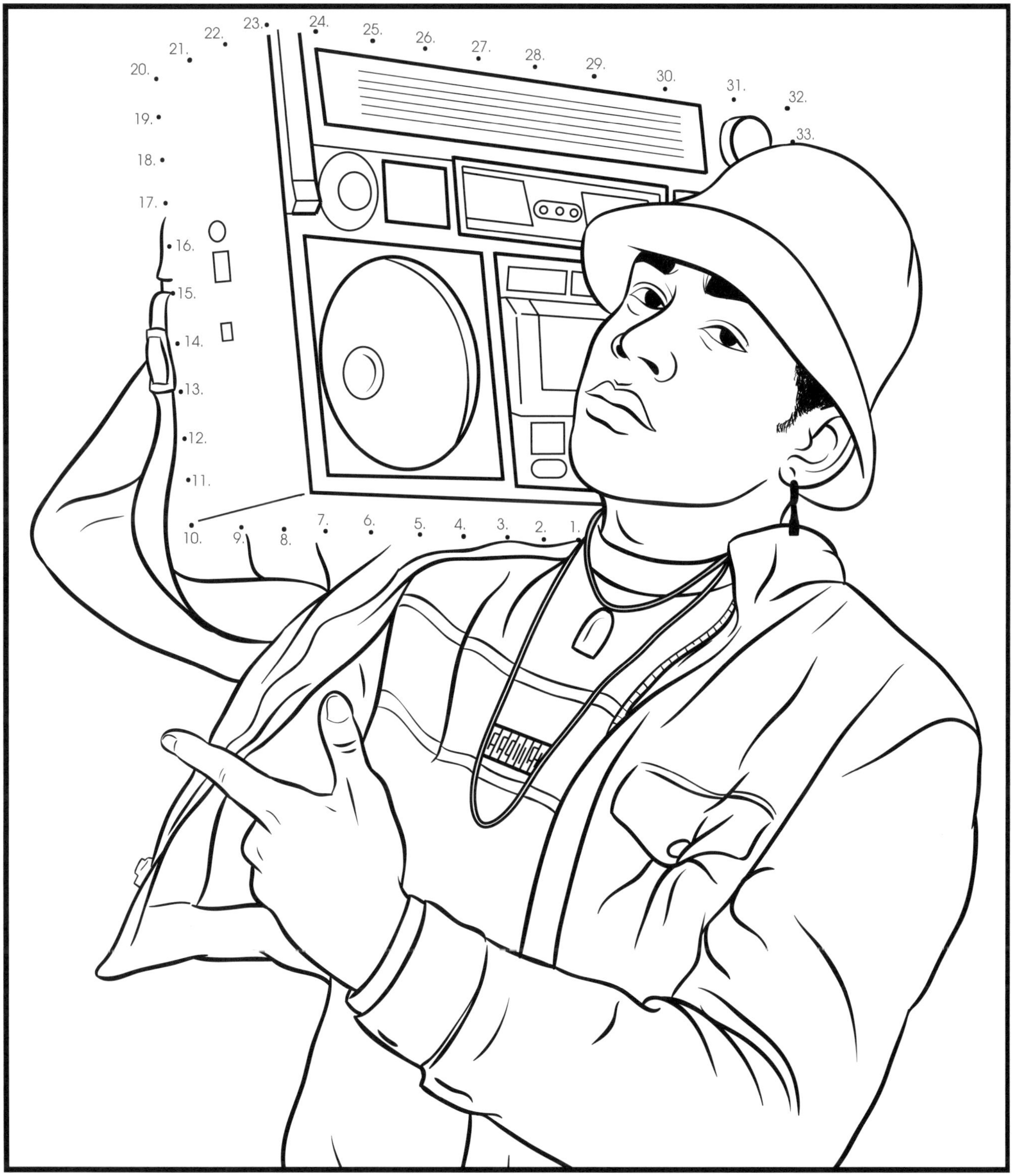
1.
2.
3.
4.
5.
6.
7.
8.
9.
10.
11.
12.
13.
14.
15.
16.
17.
18.
19.
20.
21.
22.
23.
24.
25.
26.
27.
28.
29.
30.
31.
32.
33.

LL COOL J has recorded some of the most memorable songs in rap's history, but he can't listen to any of them right now because his boombox is incomplete. Connect the dots to draw it for him.

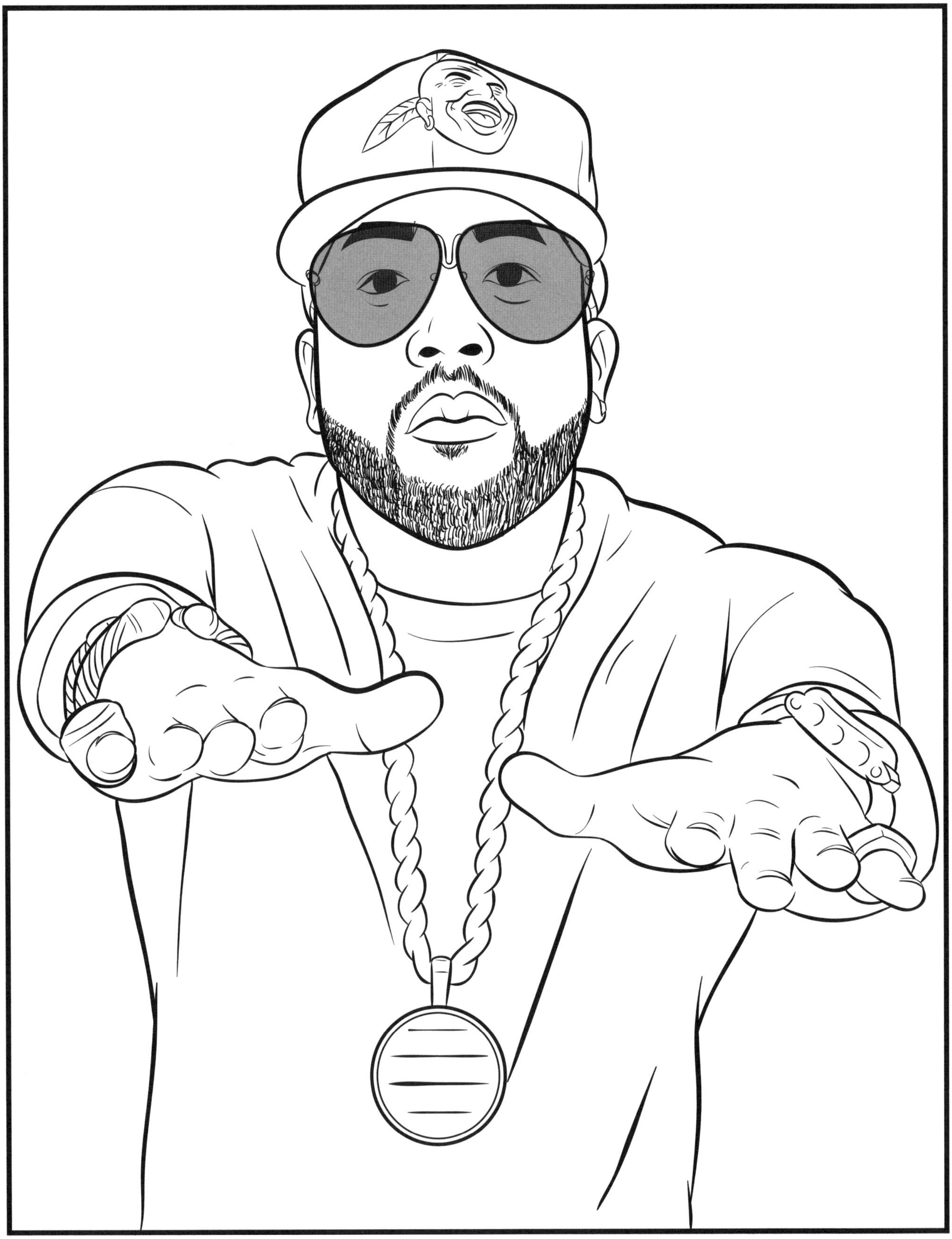

Jay Z once bragged, "I made the Yankee hat more famous than a Yankee can." Having manufactured himself into one of the most successful, most influential rappers of all time, he might've been telling the truth. Be a mogul for the day. Draw yourself in his iconic hat and glasses.

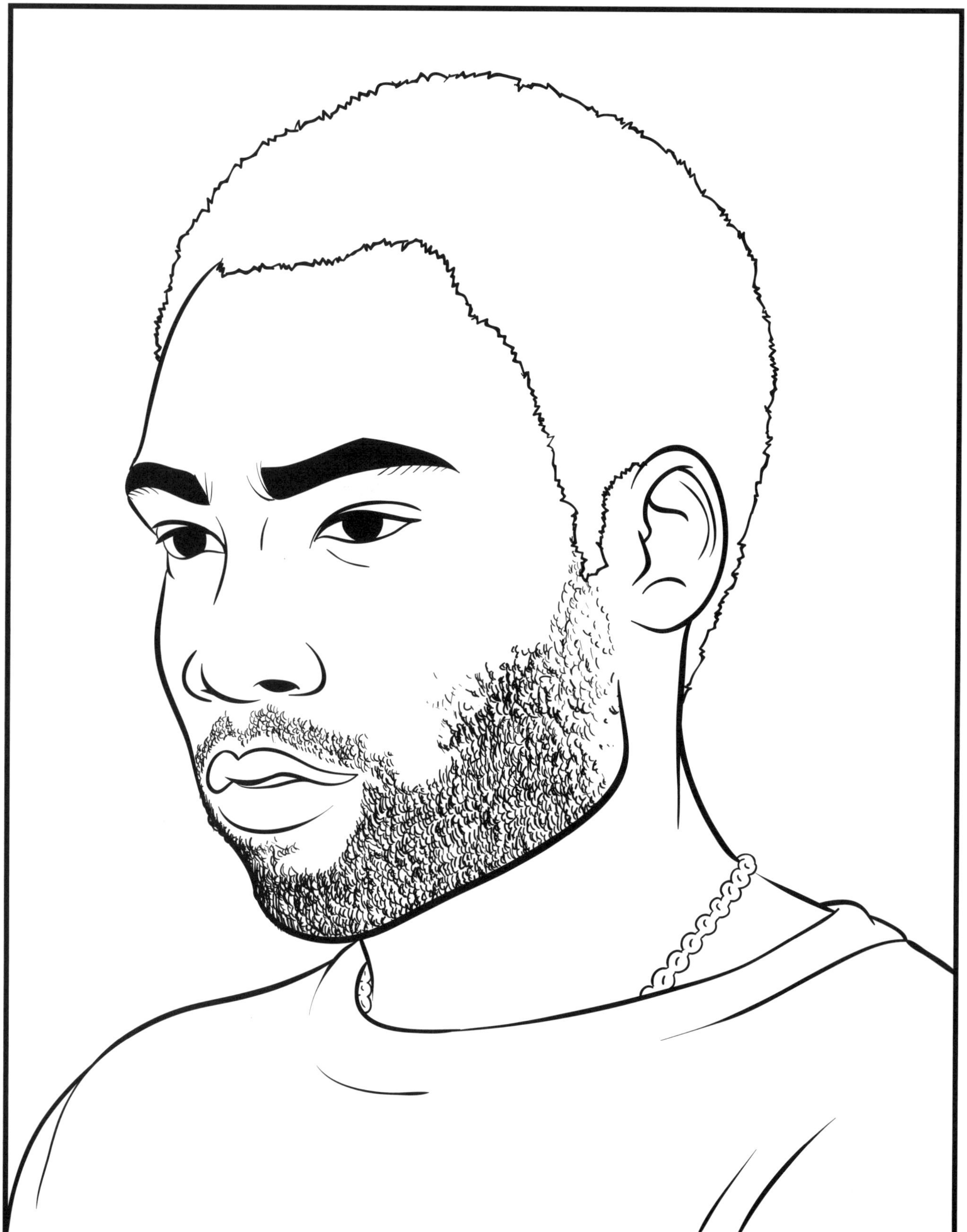

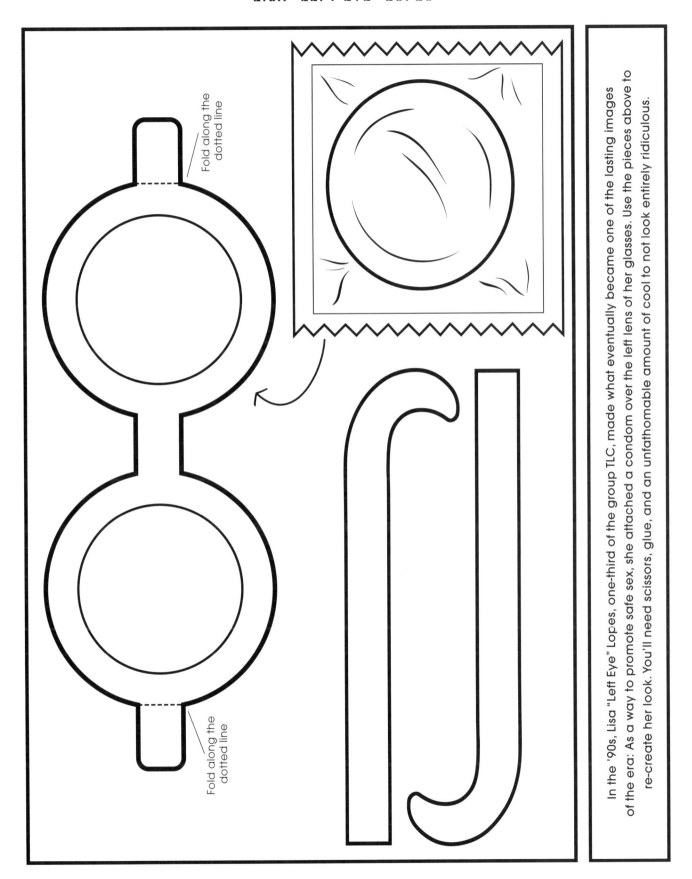

Fold along the dotted line

Fold along the dotted line

In the '90s, Lisa "Left Eye" Lopes, one-third of the group TLC, made what eventually became one of the lasting images of the era: As a way to promote safe sex, she attached a condom over the left lens of her glasses. Use the pieces above to re-create her look. You'll need scissors, glue, and an unfathomable amount of cool to not look entirely ridiculous.

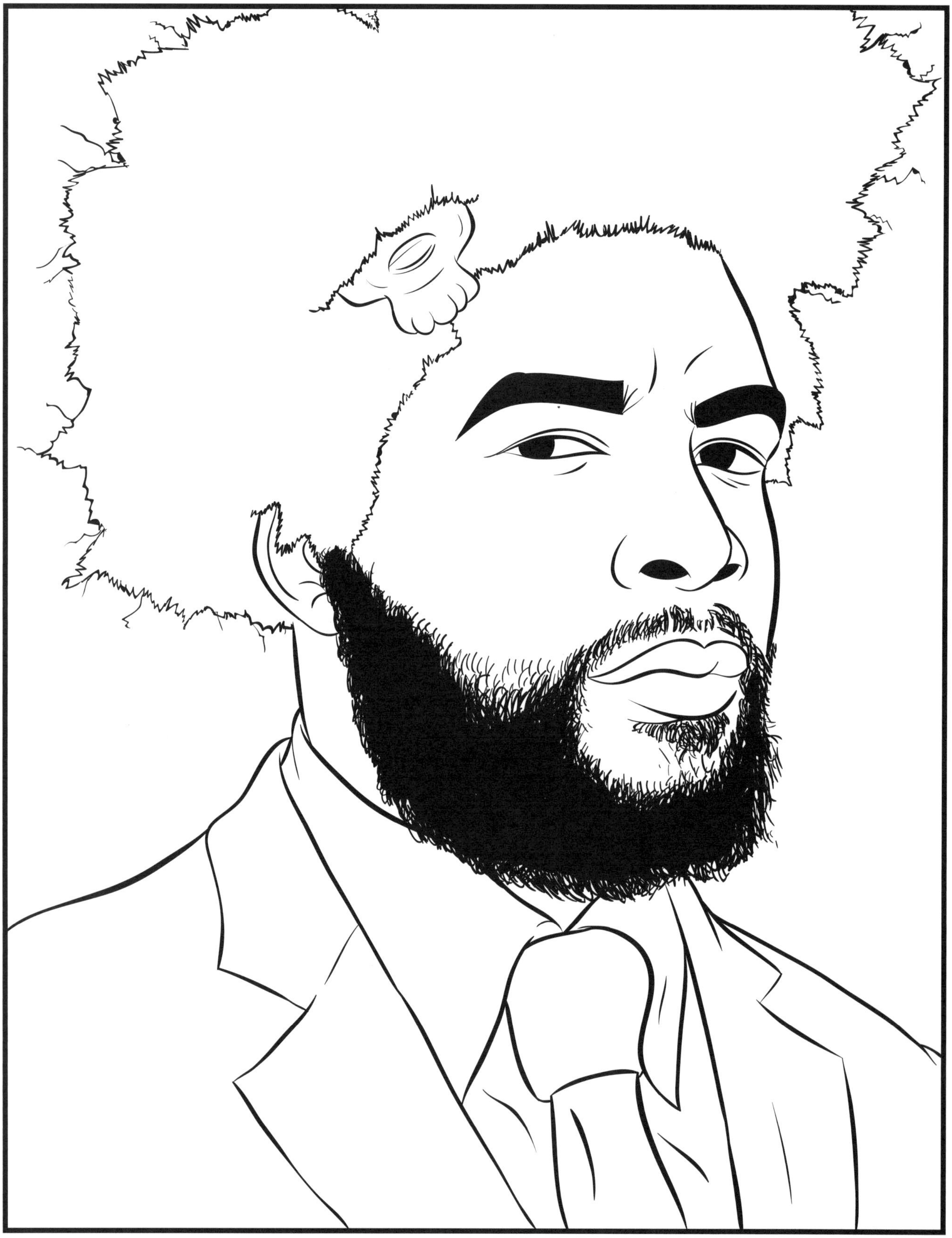

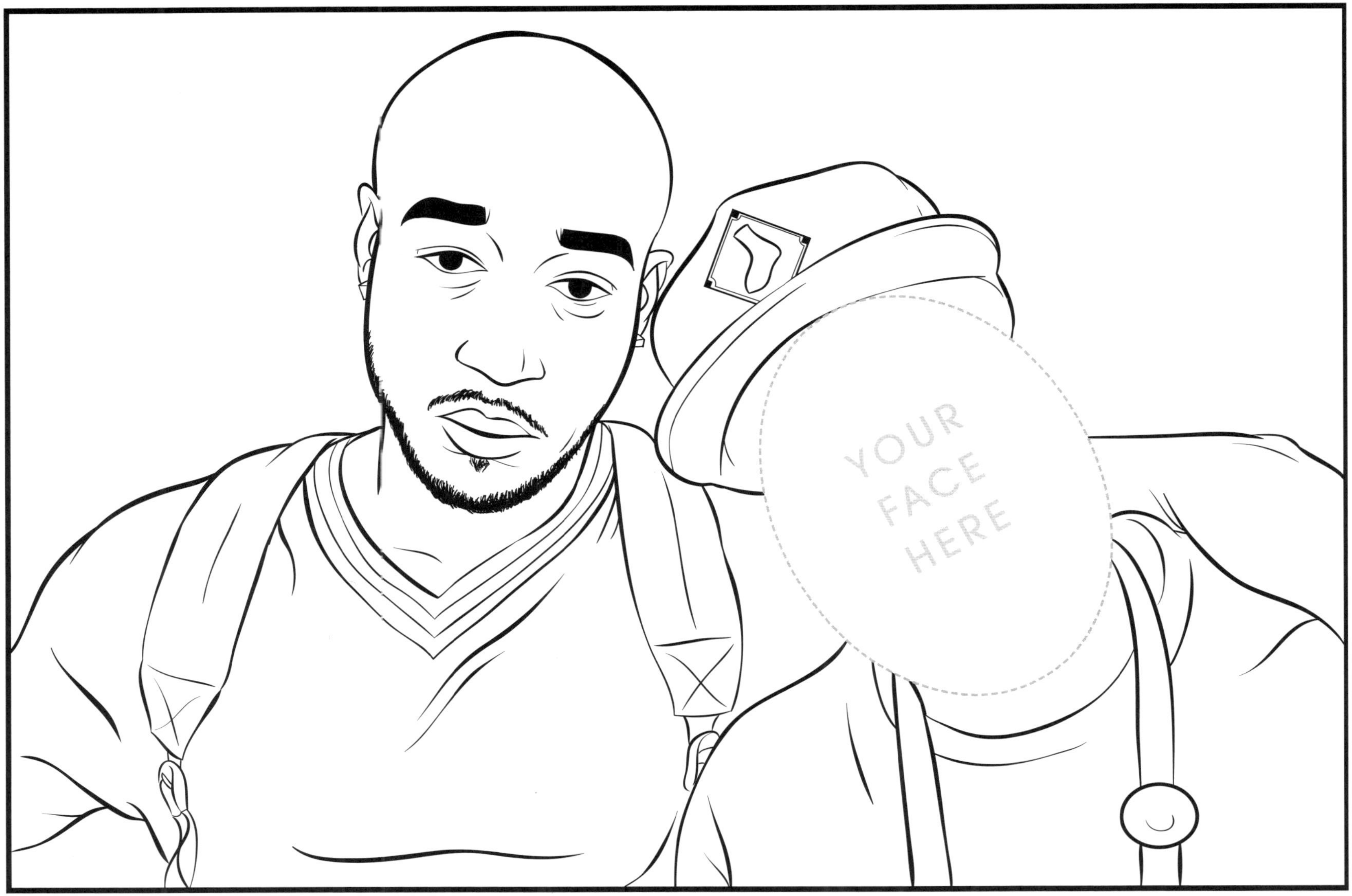
YOUR
FACE
HERE

Freddie Gibbs, Indiana's endlessly skillful rap king, is one of rap's best, most underappreciated talents. He'll be world famous soon enough. And when he is, you'll want to be able to tell everyone how you and he are cool. So paste a picture of your face on the appropriate section above. Color it. Put it in a frame. Malibooyah. You're friends with a famous rapper.

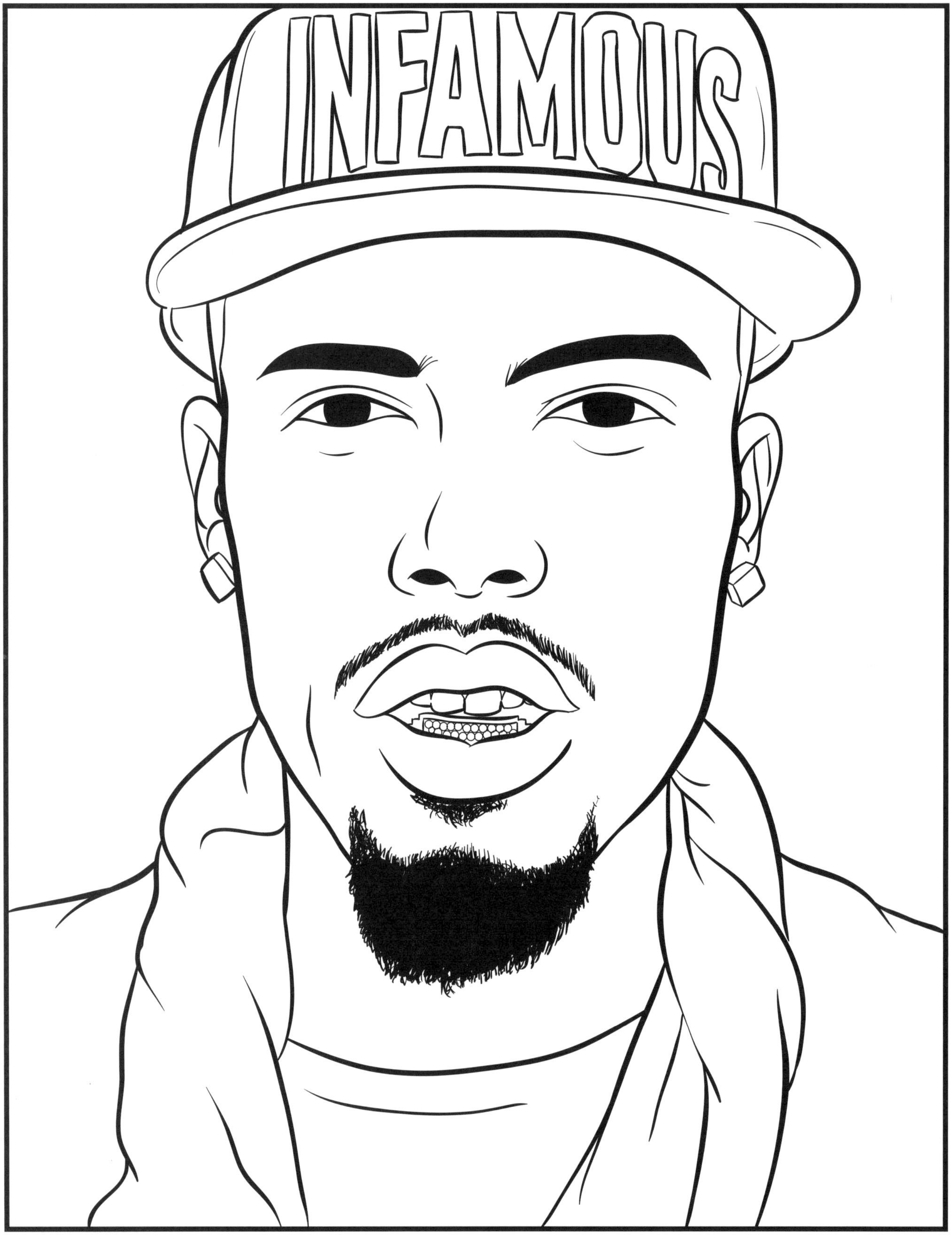
INFAMOUS

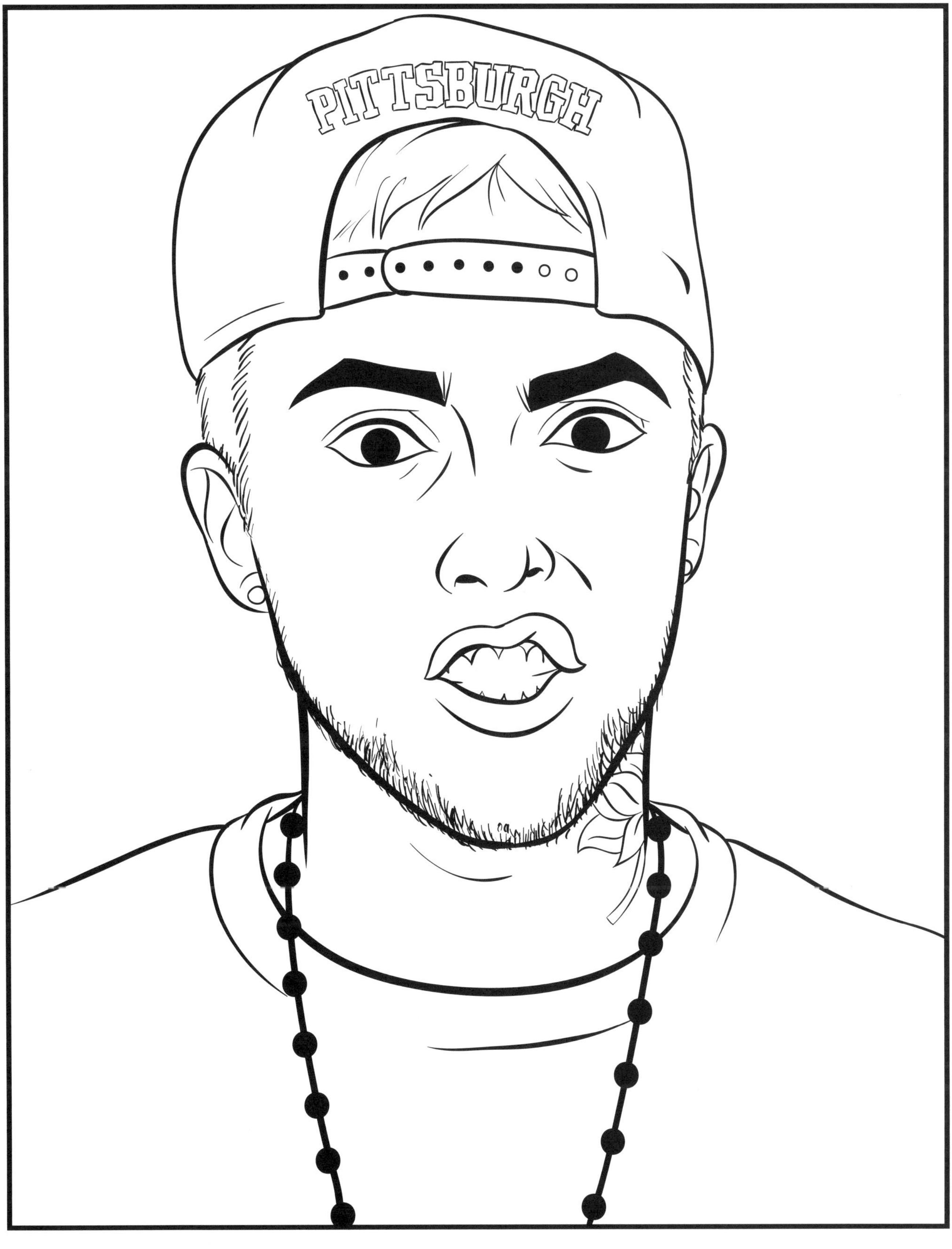
PITTSBURGH

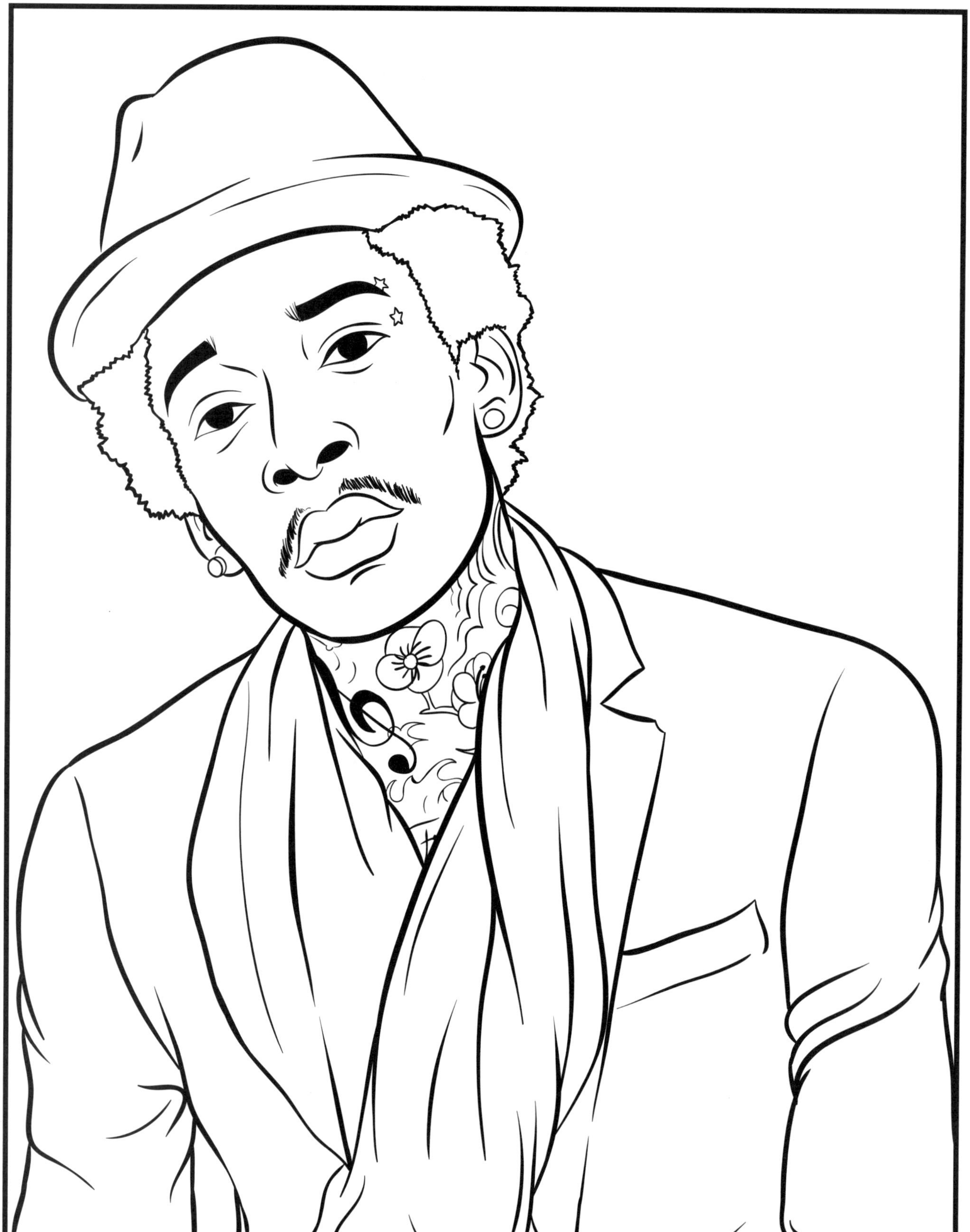

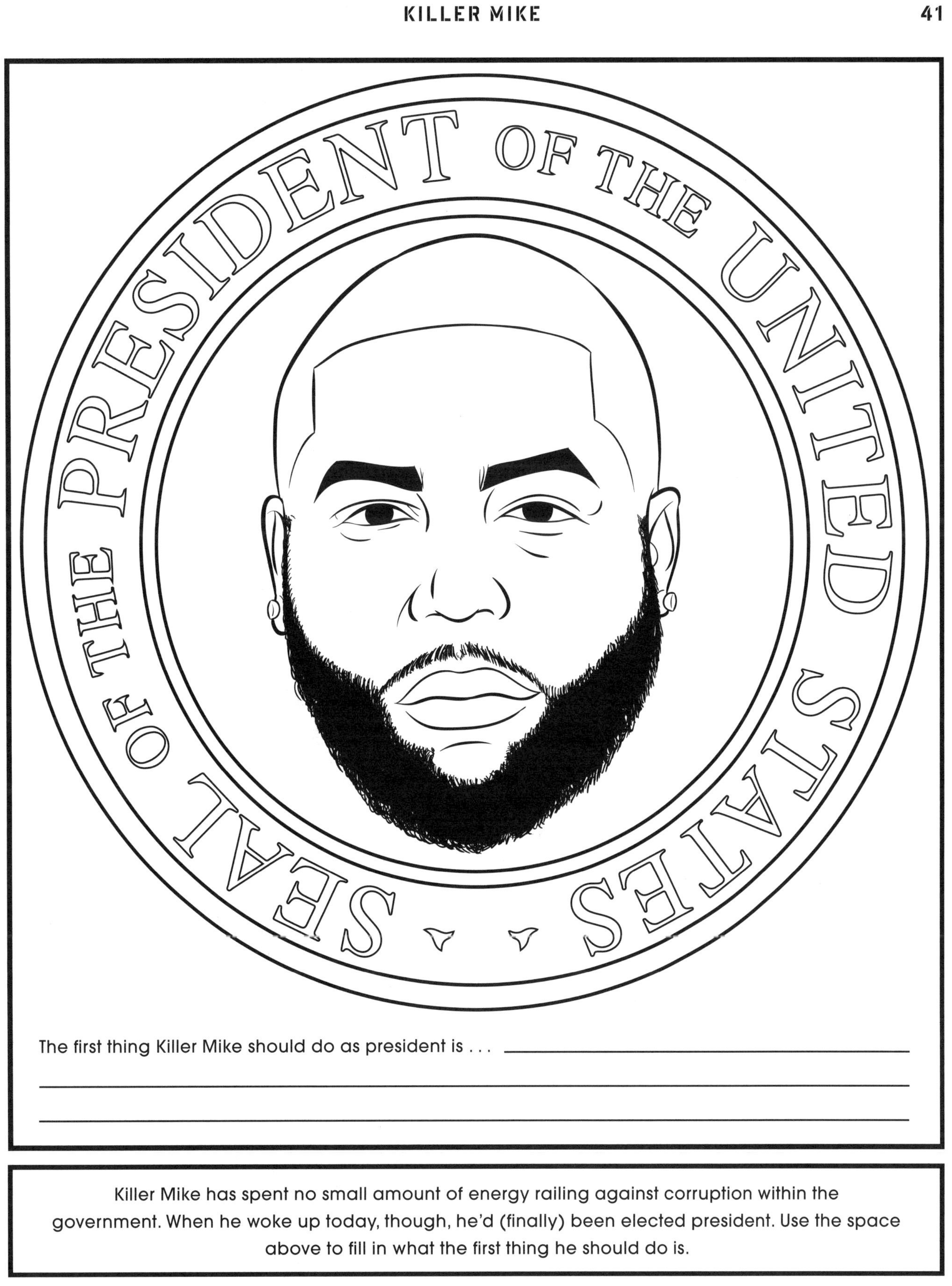
SEAL OF THE PRESIDENT OF THE UNITED STATES

The first thing Killer Mike should do as president is . . . ______________________

______________________

______________________

Killer Mike has spent no small amount of energy railing against corruption within the government. When he woke up today, though, he'd (finally) been elected president. Use the space above to fill in what the first thing he should do is.

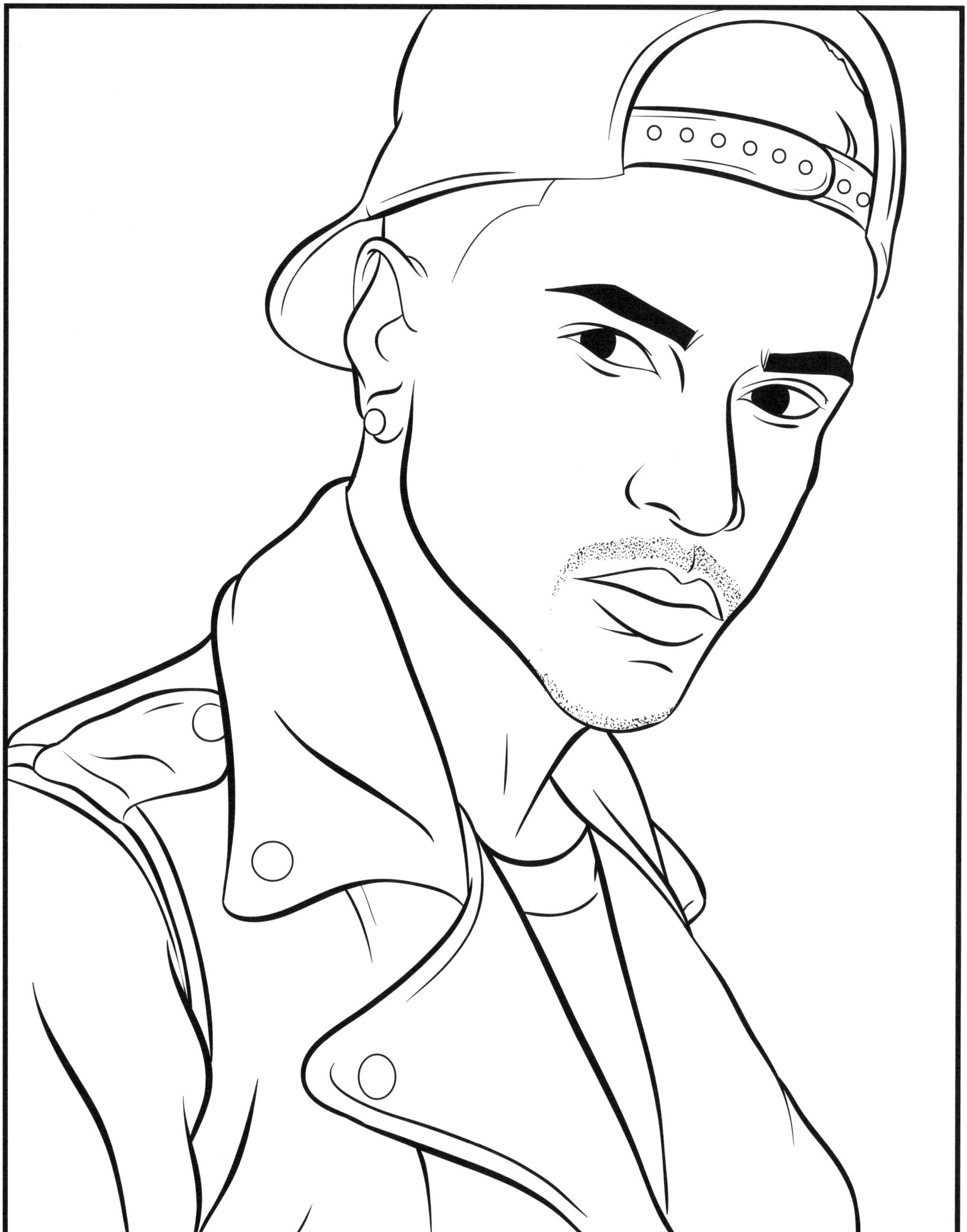

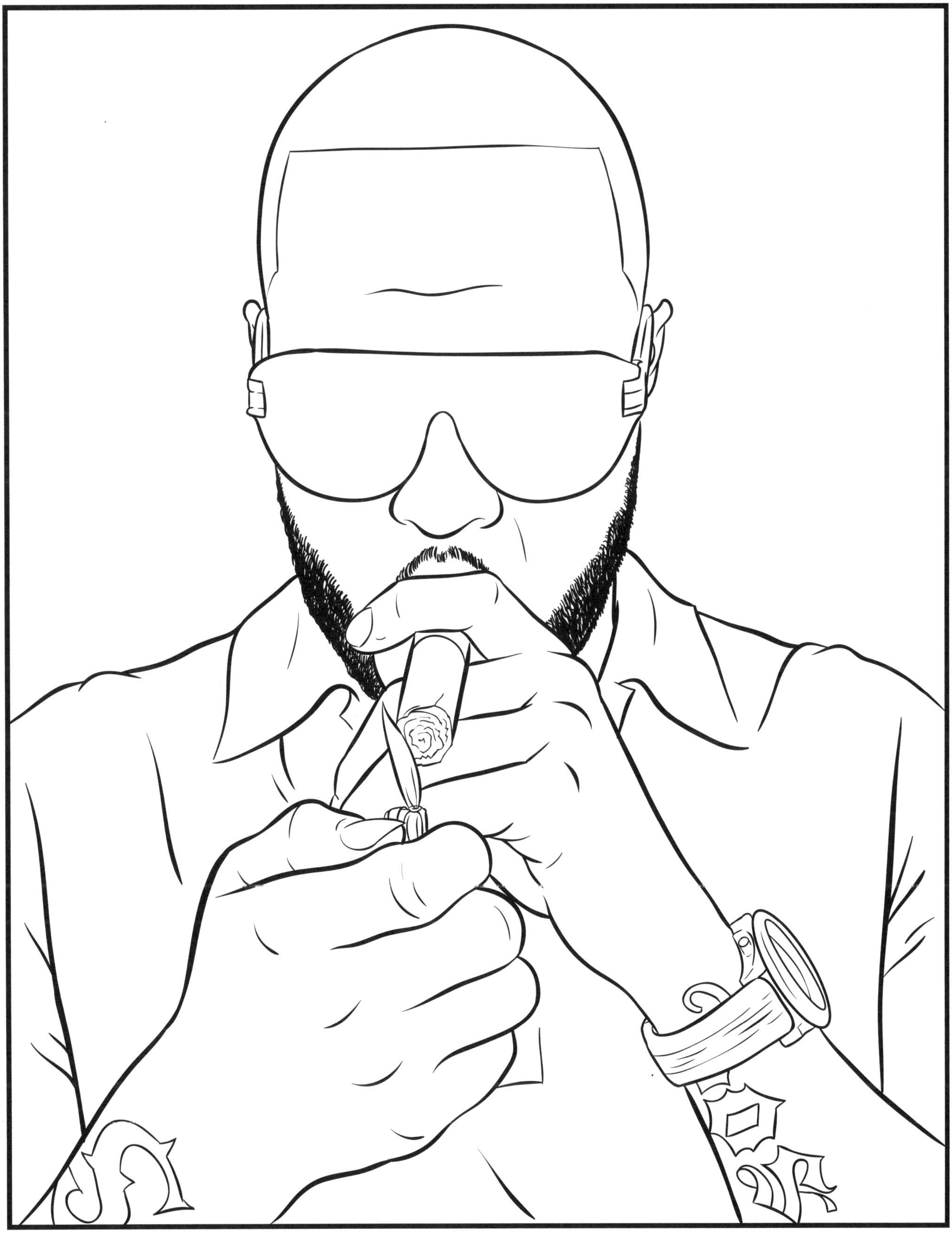

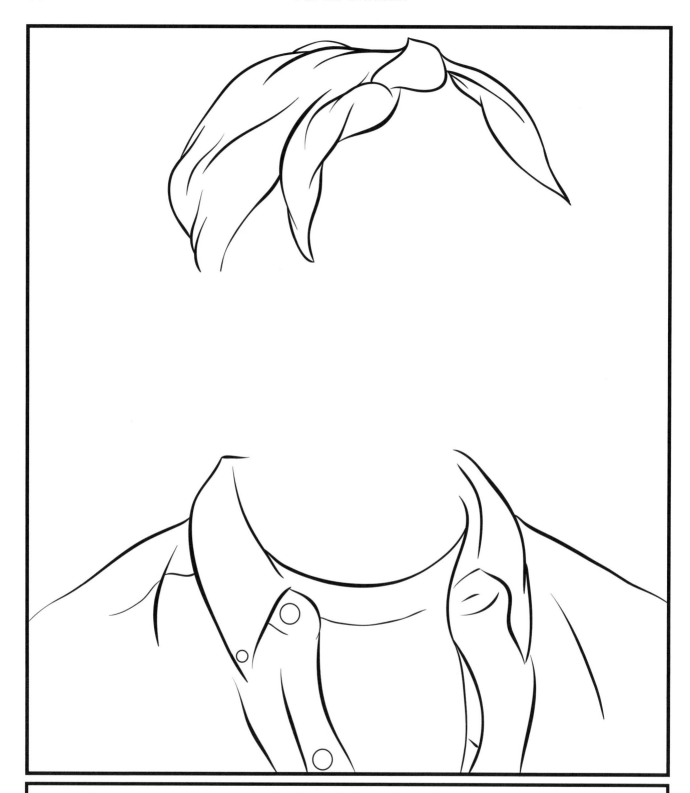

Even today, nearly a decade after his death, Tupac Shakur's cultural influence is still felt.
What other man could take a garment as innocuous as a bandanna and turn it into one of the most
important relics in music's history? You'll never be a rap legend, but you can at least pretend.
Draw yourself wearing Tupac's bandanna.

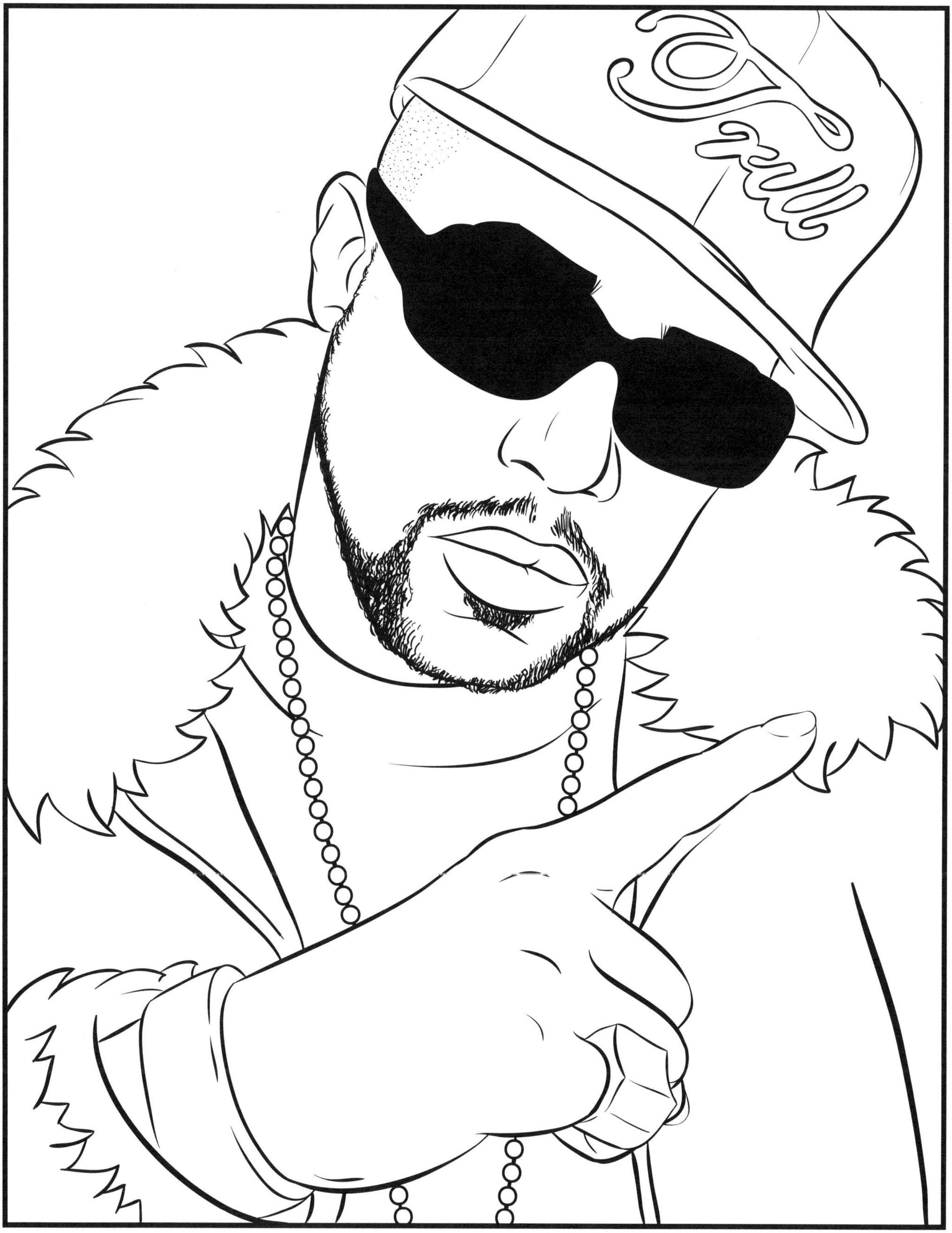
Trill

**BUN B**
One-half of UGK, one of the most influential rap groups of all time. Listen to "Murder."

**NOTORIOUS B.I.G.**
Srsly? Here, do this: Take your hand, make a fist, then punch yourself. Listen to "Juicy."

**QUEEN LATIFAH**
Maybe the greatest female rapper of them all, and definitely one of the greatest rappers of them all. Listen to "Ladies First."

**E-40**
West Coast rap cult hero and superheroically gifted neologist. Listen to "Big Ballin' with My Homies."

**DRAKE**
The single most unstoppable rapper of his generation. Listen to "Headlines."

**ACTION BRONSON**
One of the brightest spots in New York's new generation of rappers. Listen to "Big Trouble in Little China."

**WILLIE D**
The most visceral, most

intimidating member of the monumental Geto Boys. Listen to "Bald Headed Hoes."

**GZA**
From the Wu-Tang Clan. Likely has the universe's secrets typed onto a notepad app in his cell phone. Listen to "Cold World."

**TALIB KWELI**
Most often recognized as one-half of the gargantuan duo Black Star. Preternaturally cool and insightful. Listen to "Good to You."

**SCARFACE**
Scarface is the master craftsman in the Geto Boys, his booming baritone voice helping to define an entire generation of rap. Listen to "I Seen a Man Die."

**ICE-T**
One of the forefathers of gangsta rap. Also, as it turns out, a great director as well. Go watch his documentary *The Art of Rap*. Listen to "Police Story."

**KANYE WEST**
It's Kanye, bro. Kanye.

Listen to "Can't Tell Me Nothing."

**MC LYTE**
Not nearly as heralded as she should be. Was actually the first woman on the planet to release a proper full-length rap album (1988's *Lyte as a Rock*). Listen to "Rock the Party."

**CHAMILLIONAIRE**
First Houston rapper to win a Grammy. Probably not the first Houston rapper to ride dirty. Listen to "Ridin' Dirty."

**WALE**
Gained national acclaim in 2008 with a hypercreative mixtape named *A Mixtape About Nothing* that utilized a handful of Seinfeld sound bites. Listen to "The Kramer."

**TECH N9NE**
Virtuoso underground rapper. Often called "weird," though only ever as a compliment. Listen to "Poh Me Anutha."

**MACHINE GUN KELLY**
Firecracker rapper. Is responsible for a door missing from one of

Diddy's mansions. Listen to "Wild Boy."

**COMMON**
Here's what you need to know about Common: His Wikipedia has him listed as "Common (entertainer)." He is an author, an actor, a Grammy-winning rapper, and (I'd guess) a hat enthusiast. Listen to "The Light."

**DANNY BROWN**
Oddball genius rapper. Maybe the greatest hair that's ever been. Listen to "Pac Blood."

**RIFF RAFF**
The actualization of the most fun parts of the Internet. Might be a genius. Might not be a genius. Listen to "JUiCE."

**BIG K.R.I.T.**
Possesses what many would consider to be a beautiful understanding of the Southern rap aesthetic. Could be its next great. Listen to "Country Shit."

**JOE BUDDEN**
Positively fantastic at saying words that rhyme,

and most assuredly an underappreciated talent. Listen to "Things You Do."

## MACKLEMORE

Became a star after his 2012 single "Thrift Shop" popped. Has a back catalogue of solid songs, too. Listen to "Thrift Shop."

## RICK ROSS

The first rapper to ever rap about lavishness in a truly transcendent way. Fantastic. Listen to "Hustlin'."

## JEAN GRAE

A queen in underground rap and an ultra-engaging online personality. Listen to "Strikes."

## JUICY J

One-half of the beautifully trenchant duo Three 6 Mafia. Listen to "Late Night Tip."

## LUDACRIS

Part of the Atlanta rap renaissance and way more influential than he's given credit for. To wit: Did you know that he's won awards from MTV, the Screen Actor's Guild, the Grammys, and a whole host more? And all you ever want to talk about is that

video where he has mega arms. Listen to "Move Bitch."

## TRAE THA TRUTH

Southern rap savant. Might've been the first rapper to receive a city-sanctioned holiday for his community service. Listen to "Swang."

## LL COOL J

His early work in helping solidify rap as a viable branch of pop culture ("Radio," "Mama Said Knock You Out," etc) secured his place in the ultra-elite IMPORTANT RAPPERS category. Listen to "I'm Bad."

## BIG BOI

First as a member of Atlanta's godlike rap duo Outkast through 2007, and now as a dazzling solo performer, Big Boi has firmed himself as an all-timer. Listen to: ANYTHING from *Sir Lucious Left Foot: The Son of Dusty Chico*

## JAY Z

Dude. Listen to "22 Twos."

## CHILDISH GAMBINO

A rapper and a come-

dian and an actor and somehow exceptional at all three. Listen to "Lights Turned On."

## LISA "LEFT EYE" LOPES

One-third of the group TLC and also an accomplished solo artist. Listen to "I Believe In Me."

## QUESTLOVE

Not a rapper, but, I mean, he's Questlove. This could've been a book about politicos in Mexico and we'd have tried to get him. Listen to "Distortion to Static."

## FREDDIE GIBBS

So much fun. Listen to "Kush Cloud."

## B.O.B

As comfortable alongside Lil Wayne as he is alongside Hayley Williams. Listen to "Airplanes."

## MAC MILLER

Super fun and uncommonly successful; his debut studio album was the first independently distributed album since 1995's *Dogg Food* to debut at number one on Billboard's 200. Listen to "Donald Trump."

## WIZ KHALIFA

Self-made superstar, and maybe the most inherently likable rapper of all. Listen to "On My Level."

## KILLER MIKE

Does not care for the less-than-entirely-altruistic manner in which the government occasionally conducts itself in, raps really well about it. Listen to "Reagan."

## BIG SEAN

Basically just swervin' all over everyone's face. Listen to "Guap."

## SLIM THUG

Southern rap businessman. Listen to "Like a Boss."

## TUPAC SHAKUR

Come on. Listen to "Hit 'Em Up."

## PIMP C

The other half of UGK. In addition to being a brilliant producer and charismatic rapper, he is generally regarded as the greatest shit talker rap has ever seen. Listen to "Diamonds & Wood."

## ACKNOWLEDGMENTS

First, duh, thank you to Bun B. You are the GODKING. I will always remember the day that you called me and asked if I wanted to work on a book with you, and I will always remember thinking "DO NOT FUCK THIS UP" immediately afterward. You are a great rapper and an even better human. Sorry I turned your original book idea into a coloring book.

Great care was taken to make sure that everyone whose face appeared in this book was aware that their face was appearing in this book. We didn't feature anybody here that didn't give us exclusive permission to do so, and that's something we're very proud of. So, super thank you to all of the artists who agreed to participate. You all are some of the most talented people on the planet. I'm glad we're all true best friends now. Let's hang out.

To that last point, there was a whole army of wonderful and helpful people I met while coordinating this project. Thank you to the 150 or so managers, handlers, agents, assistants, and lawyers that helped line everything up. You did God's work.

Thank you to the gorgeously talented photographers that allowed us to use their photos for parts of the book, including, but not limited to, Tasha Bleu, Jesse Lirola, Glen Friedman, Mark Squires, Todd Spoth, Janette Beckman, Jonathan Mannion, Brock Fetch, and Julia Beverly. I hope you all are proud of what we were able to do with them.

Thank you to Evan Auerbach, from the wonderful rap photo tumblr Up North Trips (UpNorthTrips.com), and Barry Schwartz (from Mars or wherever you're from). Your repeated insight was invaluable. Additionally, thank you to all the rest of the talented writers and artists that I leaned on for ideas and inspiration for tumblr and the book at any point during all this, including, but not limited to, Ben Westhoff, Mike Ayers, Keith Plocek, Anthony Obi, Rob Harvilla, Andrew Nosnitsky, Brandon Soderberg, Lawrence Schlossman, Matt Sonzala, Chris Weingarten, Mark Lisanti, Rembert Browne, Paul Cantor, Jozen Cummings, Henry Adaso, David Drake, Jeff Weiss, Sascha Stone, and all the secret POTW message board weirdoes. Sorry if I missed anyone.

Thank you to Chris Gray and Margaret Downing. I am forever indebted to both of you. You two were the first people that ever trusted me to write anything of importance, and I will never pass up an opportunity to tell everyone how smart you two are and how influential you have been to me.

Thank you to Samantha Weiner, my tireless and exceptional editor from ABRAMS. I very likely emailed you nine thousand times during this process and you never once made me feel like I was anything other than important and valued. I'm certain you will always be successful at this. I hope we work together on a hundred different projects.

Thank you to my sisters, Yasminda, Nastasja, and Marie. You are all wonderful and if I ever make any money in my life I'm going to buy the biggest pants in the world so I can carry the three of you around in my pocket and protect you from everything always.

Thank you to my Marmaduke and to my Parp for pretending like you were excited that your only son became a guy that gets paid to make jokes about boners on the Internet and draw pictures of rappers. You two are marvelous and have only ever encouraged me to do what makes me happy. I hope that when I die my sons feel the same way about me that I feel about you guys.

Thank you to my goofy, beautiful, perfect sons, Bay Bear, Meechy, and The Park Show. I will love you long past when the sun runs out of energy, and I will carry you on my shoulders for rides up the stairs until my legs fail.

Thank you to all the people on the planet. If you bought this book, then I love you and you are my true best friend. If you didn't buy this book then I hate you. Just kidding. But buy the book. For real.

And thank you to my wife, my boo, my main crime partner, the most important person in my life, Larami. I am always amazed by how endlessly you support and believe in me. You have been more than I ever deserved, and I absolutely cannot wait to be a sixty-year-old man chasing you around trying to get you to make out with me. I love you.

## CREDITS

p.05 © Michael Ochs Archives/GettyImages
p.06, 17, 28 © Julia Beverly
p.07 © Mark Squires
p.08 © Brock Fetch
p.12 © Jonathan Mannion
p.13 © Glen Friedman
p.21 © Jesse Lirola
p.22 © Tasha Bleu
p.31 © Janette Beckman
p.32 © Todd Spoth

### EDITOR
Samantha Weiner

### DESIGNER
Sebit Min

### PRODUCTION MANAGER
Anet Sirna-Bruder

ISBN: 978-1-4197-1041-4
Copyright © 2013
Shea Serrano

Abrams Image books are available at special discounts when purchased in quantity for premiums and promotions as well as fundraising or educational use. Special editions can also be created to specification. For details, contact specialsales@abramsbooks.com or the address below.

**ABRAMS**
THE ART OF BOOKS SINCE 1949

115 West 18th Street
New York, NY 10011
www.abramsbooks.com